This program is good; it points out the need to repent and take accountability for one's own actions. That's just not taught anymore.

Pastor in Tennessee

I was an alcoholic/addict for twenty-two years, and have been set free, redeemed, and bought with the blood of Jesus Christ. Finding this group has helped me discover the root of my uncontrollable addictions, restore my life through Christ, and hold me accountable so that I do not return to my former ways.

Benny Jasper
Men's Group Leader

God used Addicts at the Cross in my life to unlock the Scriptures. I learned the truth about who God is and who I am. Many people in our group were moved as God's Word came to life and brothers shared with each other.

Yancy Helton

The greatest thing about Addicts at the Cross and the "step" program is that the Gospel is presented entirely and completely and simply in every meeting.

Heath Tappe
Bridge Street Mission, Wausau WI

At Addicts at the Cross, I have found my home. I have found family here and have learned to grow in Christ and in my recovery while working the steps. I'm so blessed to have found this. I have witnessed an amazing transformation in the lives of my group members since they started the Addicts at the Cross program. Our heart's desire is to know God and have an intimate relationship with Him. I cannot thank you enough for this program.

Jennifer Ortega
Gatesville, TX

The Addicts at the Cross program isn't just another program that helps you "white knuckle" your way through the steps, telling you to abstain from your addictions. This program leads you to Jesus Christ, the only one who can break the chains that bind you. Addicts at the Cross shows you how to substitute your self-centered life with a Christ-centered life, which is the key to successfully beating any and all addictions. I'm thankful for Brother Larry Skrant and his Addicts at the Cross ministry for helping me and countless others like me. I am thrilled to be able to take this program to others in my community who are battling the demons of addiction.

Kevin Lane

An effective pointer to the most powerful source of life transformation - the cross of Jesus Christ. Written by one whom Christ set free, first from sin, then from its various forms of control, including addiction. The success of this nine step study is its straight pathway into the Bible and to the cross, on which the steps travel.

Darwin Hartman
Pike Mennonite Church Lima Ohio

Larry is one of the most gifted and inspiring teachers I know. Larry has many life experiences that are penned in this book. *Addicts at the Cross* is written in such a way that the reader can sense the same inspiration as if they were sitting in a class. Each step builds one upon the other and is the most Christ-centered addiction curriculum that I know of. I have heard many men behind prison walls testify to the change that Christ has done in their lives because of going through this book.

John Yoder
Director of Carolina Chaplaincy Program

I have used the Addicts at the Cross program in a number of counseling and discipleship situations, and have found it highly effective. Larry Skrant's firsthand experiences as an addict prior to his salvation give him the unique ability to relate to those who find themselves in bondage to their sin. This study provides a clear, biblically-based pathway to lasting freedom from sin and addiction that can only be found in Jesus Christ.

Steve Williams, PhD, DMin

We really appreciate this program.
Ohio Prison Chaplain

This program is great and addresses the root causes of any addiction.
Church Member in Alabama

I am interested in information about starting an Addicts at the Cross program here in my hometown. Your program helped me more than you will ever know.
Former Inmate

Even though there are other "step" programs out there, none of those place a relationship with God as the complete and only answer.
Sheila Wilkinson

Because of Addicts at the Cross, I can honestly say for the first time in my life that I know what it's like to have faith, family, and friends!
Donna G.

ADDICTS at the CROSS

A CHRISTIAN 9-STEP PROGRAM

LARRY SKRANT

ANEKO
PRESS

Visit Larry's website: www.changedlivesministries.org

Addicts at the Cross – Larry Skrant

Copyright © 2016

First edition published 2012

All scripture is from the King James Version

Cover Design: Natalia Hawthorne, BookCoverLabs.com

eBook Icon: Icons Vector/Shutterstock

Editors: Paul Miller and Sheila Wilkinson

Printed in the United States of America

Aneko Press – *Our Readers Matter*™

www.anekopress.com

Aneko Press, Life Sentence Publishing, and our logos are trademarks of

Life Sentence Publishing, Inc.
203 E. Birch Street
P.O. Box 652
Abbotsford, WI 54405

SELF-HELP / Substance Abuse & Addictions / Alcohol

Paperback ISBN: 978-1-62245-440-2

eBook ISBN: 978-1-62245-441-9

Big Book ISBN: 978-1-62245-438-9

10 9 8 7 6 5 4 3 2 1

Available where books are sold

Contents

This book is dedicated to my sister, Sandra Caperton, LISW-S, LCDC III. "There will be no recovery without spirituality," she said to me. When she told me she was going to die, I asked her if she was okay with that. Without any hesitation she replied, "Yes, I love Jesus and Jesus loves me." There is no doubt as to who my sister's higher power was and is. I look forward to our next meeting.

About the Founder

My name is Larry Skrant. I am a member of the First Baptist Church in Spencer, Ohio, an ordained minister, the director of Changed Lives Ministries, and the founder of Addicts at the Cross. Before that I was 324-242. Before that I was 282-320. And before that I was 230-915. Those are prison numbers. To the state of Ohio, I was a three-time loser. To society, I was beyond salvaging. To all, including myself, I was beyond hope.

During my third stay in prison, I became so convinced that there was no hope for me that I made the decision to cut off all communication with my family. One year later, I received a letter in a little girl's handwriting, written in block letters with crayon. The letter simply read, "Dear Dad, my name is Stephanie. Do you remember me?" A little girl should not have to write such a letter to her father. The Lord used that letter to convict me of my sins. In my prison cell, I fell to my knees and called on His name. At that moment, I was saved and spiritually set free. Several years later, I would be set free again. Fourteen years before my anticipated release date, I was physically set free as I walked out of prison with a new heart and a new message.

My position as founder and director of Changed Lives Ministries (a gospel-preaching ministry) has opened up unique opportunities for me to share the gospel, not only in this country but around the world in places like Ireland, England, and Africa. I was particularly blessed to take part in a debate at the University of Dublin. I believe the gospel of Jesus Christ can make a bad man good and a good man better. It can alter human nature, and it can change a person's life. I believe that because mine is a life that has been changed.

A very special thank you to Sarah Sellers, who provided the inspiration and motivation needed to complete this book.

About Addicts at the Cross

Addicts at the Cross is a 9-step Christian program that deals with the root problems of addiction from a biblical point of view. This spiritual formation program focuses on a higher power. We believe that higher power to be Christ. It is important to note that we are not the only program that deals with addictions, nor do we deal with the physical side effects of addiction. Hospitals and treatment centers with trained professionals are much better equipped than we are to deal with those issues. In all cases, if people are still using or having serious withdrawal issues, we recommend that they seek help from these types of treatment centers. Once addicts are dried out or separated from their addiction, we can address the causes of the addiction and offer an alternative lifestyle with Christ at the center.

How many witnesses does it take to put a man in prison? Probably one credible person would do the trick. We could certainly provide thousands and thousands of credible people today as well as throughout the ages who would testify that Jesus Christ radically changed their lives for the better; yet the world still denies the life-changing power of the gospel. "Where are the clinical studies?" is the question most often asked by the naysayers whose worldly education encourages them to denounce the evidence of things unseen. Our clinic, though, is not a cross section of people in some sterile controlled environment where percentages can easily be manipulated; no, our clinic is the world, where we have seen healing take place, lives saved, families restored, and pain and suffering alleviated by the power of God's Word. We offer as proof our own changed lives and the changed lives of God's people throughout the ages.

Whenever I teach in prisons, juvenile centers, or addiction centers, I always ask this question: "How many of you are here because you were living in accord with the Bible?" I have yet to see one hand raised in the affirmative. My follow-up question is always this: "Shouldn't that tell you something?"

I am not saying that our program is the only one that works. I am not saying this program will work for everyone (even though I believe it would if certain conditions are met). What we are offering here is an alternative lifestyle that enables us to live our lives free from addiction. Isn't that the goal of all addiction programming?

We cannot deny that Alcoholics Anonymous has saved the lives of many people. That program, with its time-honored steps, was the model I used in developing the Addicts at the Cross program. I am also grateful for the ministry of Alcoholics for Christ. That, too, is a great program, and I also used it as a model; but for the most part, other than the step outline, this work is original, and I pray it will be life-changing for those who choose to use it.

What I have written here I refer to as a connect-the-dot program. I have personally been to many recovery meetings, and I never understood the concept of what it meant to "work the steps." No one had ever shown me how to do that. What I have attempted to do here is to offer a program that actually allows us to work through the steps while meeting together as a group. By doing so, we not only begin to understand how to work the steps, but we also begin to understand why the steps are necessary in the first place. By working through the steps together, we come to an overall understanding of what it means to be a Christian.

Once we understand who we are in Christ, it becomes increasingly more difficult for us to slide back into the abyss of our addiction. Our habits change, our friends change, and our lifestyles change. With these changes, we develop a new sense of accountability. We learn to resist anything or anyone who would take this new life from us, and we are free at last to live the life God had intended for us all along. As confirmed in my own life, my hope is that all who enter this program would come to the realization of what is written in 1 Corinthians 2:9: *Eye hath not seen, nor ear heard, neither have entered into the heart of man, the things which God hath prepared for them that love him.*

God bless you.

Sincerely,

Larry Skrant

Note – *Biblical counselors do not believe God intended to give his church the Bible and then make them wait 1,900 years for real help to come with the advent of modern psychology. The Word of God offers living, practical, and profound help that makes sense to people, that understands their problems, and that points to the power of the living Christ for change. When biblical counselors use the Word of God, they are not operating at a deficit but are offering the kind of relevant, caring, and practical wisdom that is available in no other source.*

Heath Lambert

A Theology of Biblical Counseling

Preface

It was summer and I was standing near the end of a long line of inmates going into the chow hall at Lorain Correctional Institution in Ohio. Lorain is a processing center, and I was waiting to be transferred to a parent institution where I would serve out the remainder and largest portion of my prison sentence. This was during the time of my second prison number. As we inched forward, I noticed a commotion going on toward the front of the line. I thought there might be a fight. Fights erupting among inmates standing in line for any period of time were common.

Waiting in line often resulted in someone getting frustrated and then saying or doing something to which someone else objected, and just like that, individuals or even groups of individuals would be throwing punches. This time, however, no guards ran to break up anything, so whatever was going on toward the front of the line was not a fight.

As I stepped out of line to get a better look, I realized that what was causing the stir was a herring gull (also known as a sea gull). This bird kept staggering up to an inmate in line and following the man as the line moved. I had never seen a gull act like that before; daring to draw so close to a human being was something a gull just normally would not do. I watched as the inmate reached to pick it up, but the bird immediately backed away. This drama played out for some time until the man being approached faked a turning movement away from the bird and then twisted back suddenly, snatching it up. Obviously, the bird was in a weakened condition, so it could not move very fast and did not fly away.

Curiosity got the best of me. I risked the ire of fellow inmates and walked toward the front of the line to see what was really going on between the inmate and the herring gull. It was then I saw the fish lure in the bird's beak. The lure was of the spoon variety. It was oblong in shape, concave in body, and made out of shiny metal with treble hooks at the end. This apparatus had effectively snagged the bird through both the upper and lower parts of the beak. How it got there is anybody's guess, but clearly the gull could neither eat nor drink. No wonder it was weak and staggering. How long it had been in that condition one could only imagine.

I watched the inmate remove the lure from the bird's beak and then gently release the gull into the air. It was only able to fly a few feet before it landed in the grassy area right outside the walkways leading in and out of the chow hall. The prison rule is "Don't Feed the Birds!" but everyone coming out of the chow hall was throwing bread to the gull. One man who worked in the kitchen brought out a pan of water. The bird ate and drank, and after we were all locked in for the night, it left.

The bird is gone, but the memory of that event lingers with me still. There are some things I have learned from that episode that I would like to share with you. I look back on that whole scenario and now apply it spiritually. Against all instincts raging to the contrary, that herring gull seemed to know that a human being could help it. How could that be? Certainly a bird has no cognitive powers of reasoning. The Bible says there was a time when man walked with God in the garden of Eden. All was in harmony when God appointed man to be the steward of His creation. Could it be, somewhere deep within the genetic makeup of that bird, that the memory remained of those long-ago-and-longed-for days when man was a friend and a caretaker? On that summer day, all the bird's instincts screamed that man is the enemy, but this gull was dying and it knew where to find help. Nevertheless, when the inmate reached out to it, the bird would back away.

Are we not all like that in our lost state? We have this trace of a memory of God. We have this cavern within us that only He can fill. Sin has impaled us and we are dying. Our hunger cannot be satisfied and our thirst cannot be quenched. We know God can save us, but our fleshly instincts cry out against Him. We fiercely dodge all help offered by the One whose help we desperately need.

Dear reader, our Father in heaven wants to be your friend and caretaker. He does not want you to perish, but wants you to live. He sent His Son into the world not to judge you, but that through Him (Jesus) you might be saved.

Jesus is reaching out to you. Please do not persist in backing away from Him. Day after day this world seeks to consume you. You begin to weaken, to stagger, and to fall. Dear sinner, do not die in your sins. Allow Jesus to pick you up in His loving arms. Allow Him to feed you with the bread of life and to quench your thirst with His living water. You will never regret turning to Him. He will renew your strength and you will rise up with wings as eagles. You will run and not be weary. You will walk and never faint (Isaiah 40:31). This is His promise to you, and He who created all things never lies.

The 9 Steps

We respectfully acknowledge that the nine steps presented herein are based on the time-proven steps used with much success in the great programs of Alcoholics Anonymous and Alcoholics for Christ. The main difference is an emphasis on the power of God for those who come to the cross.

Basic Concept – God has a plan and a purpose for my life, and that plan is revealed to me through His Holy Word. I acknowledge the Bible to be my ultimate guide for laying the groundwork which will enable me to live a life free from addiction.

1. Admit – I admit that my life is not my own and is beyond my ability to manage or control. I have become powerless over the substance or substances that I have abused. I acknowledge my need for God to set me free from all the things in this world that have me ensnared and prevent me from being the person God created me to be.

2. Believe – I believe that the God I need to restore my life and make me whole is to be found in the person of Jesus Christ, the Word who was with God, who is God, and who became flesh and dwelt among us (John 1:1, 14).

3. Decide – I have decided to turn from the things of the past (repent) and to ask Jesus to be lord and manager of my life (surrender).

4. Search – I have made an honest search and moral inventory of myself, and seek to eliminate that which is not in accord with God's will for my life.

5. Acknowledge – Before God, others, and myself, I acknowledge my inventory to be true. I now begin to use the information from my inventory, formulating a plan that will result in a life set free from addiction.

6. Change – I am willing to change and to allow God to change me.

7. Ask – I humbly ask God to forgive me and to change me through the power of His Holy Spirit.

8. Restore – I have made a list of all the people my actions have or may have affected/damaged, and I ask myself, "How can I make this right?"

9. Pursue – Daily, I seek to know and live out God's will, plan, **and purpose for my life.**

The Basics

The main purpose in our meeting together is to grow in our knowledge of Christ and to acknowledge our need for Him. By doing so, we increase our fellowship with God and with one another. This will result in our being accountable to God and to one another as the body of Christ. Just as iron sharpens iron, we need to lift up and support each other. God truly desires us to be whole. He wants to heal us by restoring us to a right relationship with Him. When we put into practice the principles set forth in these steps, we open ourselves up to the transforming power of God's Word, knowing in our heart of hearts that God's Word will not return to Him void. It will accomplish those changes that we so desperately need and desire. God's plan for us is beyond our understanding and surpasses all that we can ever imagine; for it is written, *Eye hath not seen, nor ear heard, neither have entered into the heart of man, the things which God hath prepared for them that love Him* (1 Corinthians 2:9).

Addicts at the Cross groups, like most other groups, will tend to take on the characteristics of their leaders and/or the denomination that is most heavily represented in the group. However, addicts are mainly non-denominational, and our program should be as well. Our goal is to teach biblical principles which, when applied, will result in lives being changed. Our goal is also to promote the gospel at every meeting. Respectfully, we leave denominational issues to the local church.

Program Goals

- To establish a personal relationship with Jesus Christ.
- To live a life free from addiction.
- To see families restored and healed.
- To eliminate the possibility of "future victims" (victims who might have been but will never be, because God changed a heart and renewed a mind).
- To establish a support/accountability group.

PRAYER – Open the meeting with prayer, asking God to prepare our hearts and open our minds for what He would have us receive through the study of His Word.

WELCOME – Greet members and guests. Give a brief statement about Addicts at the Cross, and if desired, introduce any new persons. Announcements can be made at this time.

MUSIC MINISTRY – While this is optional, a time of group singing and/or sharing (vocally or instrumentally) by those who are musically gifted can serve to prepare us for what God wants to do in the meeting. This should not exceed fifteen minutes. It is not our goal to promote any individual or group.

OPENING REMARKS – An assigned volunteer will share a Scripture reading at this time or whatever God has put on his heart concerning the particular step to be discussed. This should not exceed five minutes.

PERSONAL SHARING – Ask: "Has anyone seen God working in your life this week?" We need to develop an attitude of gratitude toward God. We can do this through sharing what God has done in our lives. The duration of this segment is entirely left to the prompting of the Holy Spirit.

BEGIN THE MEETING – Meetings should last no longer than one hour. The overall program should not last longer than one-and-a-half hours. The group leader has the responsibility to ensure this.

Lead In/The Bible is our Owner's Manual /Statements of Truth

Note: In the first verse of Genesis (*In the beginning God created the heaven and the earth*), the author made no attempt to prove the existence of God but instead stated it as a given fact. In the same way, we will not be teaching a course on apologetics here. We believe the Bible is the Word of God and the following truths to be self-evident.

Truths:
You cannot understand the Bible without divine revelation.

> *Then opened He their understanding, that they might understand the scriptures.* (Luke 24:45)

> *Howbeit, when he, the Spirit of truth, is come, he will guide you into all truth.* (John 16:13)

The Bible is God's written Word, given to man so that man might relate to God. This written Word points us to and merges with the Word that became flesh (John 1:14), taking on the likeness of man (Philippians 2:7).
  Discuss some of the ways they are similar.

NOTES

Commonalities between the Bible and Jesus: (This is not intended to be a complete list.)

The Bible is God's written Word — Jesus is the Word incarnate.

The Bible is Jewish in origin — Jesus is a descendant of Abraham.

God's Word is eternal (1 Peter 1:25) — Jesus is God eternal.

The Bible is a book about humanity — Jesus is the Son of Man.

The Bible is for all people — Jesus is for all people.

The Bible is for all generations — Jesus is for all generations.

The Bible holds forth the Word of life — Jesus is the life.

God's Word is true — Jesus is the truth.

God's Word points the way — Jesus is the Way.

God's Word is a lamp — Jesus is the Light of the world.

The Bible is infinite in its knowledge — Jesus is omniscient.

God's Word will accomplish what He pleases — The Father was pleased with the Son.

Mankind sought to destroy the Bible — Mankind sought to destroy Christ.

Q. Can you think of anything that the written Word has in common with Jesus that is not listed above? Do you think these things are coincidences?

All scripture is given by inspiration of God, and is profitable for doctrine, for reproof, for correction, for instruction in righteousness: that the man of God may be perfect, thoroughly furnished unto all good works. (2 Timothy 3:16-17)

For the word of God is quick, and powerful, and sharper than any two-edged sword, piercing even to the dividing asunder of soul and spirit, and of the joints and marrow, and is a discerner of the thoughts and intents of the heart. (Hebrews 4:12)

The Bible is true. The truth never changes.

Note: Unlike man's truth which is relative and varies with cultural views or with who is in power, God's Word remains the same. Today, man's truth seems relative to whatever the polls say. Polling can be misleading. Polls can be taken to solicit a specific response. Also, as was the case in biblical days and is still the case today, the majority can be wrong. The Bible is time-tested and proven. God's truth will remain long after man's version of the truth has passed away.

For I am the LORD, I change not. (Malachi 3:6a)

Jesus Christ the same yesterday, and to day, and for ever. (Hebrews 13:8)

God forbid: yea, let God be true, but every man a liar; as it is written, That thou mightest be justified in thy sayings, and mightest overcome when thou art judged. (Romans 3:4)

For the word of the LORD is right; and all his works are done in truth. (Psalm 33:4)

Sanctify them through thy truth: thy word is truth. (John 17:17)

The Bible is life-changing. An acronym we can use is BIBLE: **B**asic **I**nstructions **B**efore **L**eaving **E**arth.

Note: Millions of people down through the ages have testified that God's Word has miraculously transformed them. Some have testified with their very lives that God's Word is true. God's Word changes us from the inside out. So why do we doubt it?

Thy word is a lamp unto my feet, and a light unto my path. (Psalm 119:105)

As for God, his way is perfect: the word of the LORD is tried: he is a buckler to all those that trust in him. (Psalm 18:30)

And thine ears shall hear a word behind thee, saying, This is the way, walk ye in it, when ye turn to the right hand, and when ye turn to the left. (Isaiah 30:21)

Wherewithal shall a young man cleanse his way? by taking heed thereto according to thy word. (Psalm 119:9)

Points to Consider Before You Begin to Implement the Steps

A good working definition of addiction is "A constellation of unbiblical habits of thinking and acting that have become a lifestyle" (from Steve Gallagher's book, *At the Altar of Sexual Idolatry*).

1. I have been asked, "Why another step program?" Clearly, I could have presented the same material in another format. However, I did not want our meetings to resemble a church meeting, nor did I want those who attend the meetings to feel preached to. Although I am a great supporter of the local church, I realize that most addicts feel uncomfortable in that kind of setting. I also know that most

NOTES

addicts have attended either AA (Alcoholics Anonymous) or NA (Narcotics Anonymous) and are familiar with and comfortable with that type of programming. I decided to start with what they know. I wanted to meet them where they are.

2. The definition of ministry is to meet people where they are and take them to where God wants them to be. Therefore, we need to make sure the gospel is presented in an understandable way at every meeting. Some people may attend only one meeting. We get one shot at these people, and it is our Christian obligation to make sure they hear the gospel.

3. The two words an addict hates hearing are *accountability* and *responsibility*. We need to stress those concepts, along with the concepts of rehabilitation and restitution. We should not encourage shortcuts. We do not want people looking for the easy way out of their problems. We want them to confront and deal with their problems in a way that is in accord with the Word of God.

4. Avoid being an enabler. Listen for signs of pride and self-centeredness. Listen for signs of blame-shifting, rationalization, and minimizing. We should help addicts confront themselves.

5. Our goal is to tear down the addict's old identity by confronting the addict with the Word of God. We can then offer addicts a clear presentation of who they could and should be in Christ. In helping addicts see both identities clearly, they will desire the new person over the old when confronted with the temptation to return to the old lifestyle.

6. Stick with the steps. Do not allow the meeting to get sidetracked.

7. Respond to all answers in an encouraging way. Iron sharpens iron. Do not be condescending. You might learn something as well. For some addicts, it takes a great deal of courage to raise their hand; we need to honor that. Young Christians can be bruised easily. We do not want to hurt them.

8. Do all things out of love. Remember the condition you were in when Jesus rescued you.

9. I did not include answers to all the questions in the book. This leaves room for the group and the leader to work out the answers. You will be surprised how much more easily the answers are understood, remembered, and applied when worked out in this manner. This also leaves more latitude for the leader to direct the discussion under the guidance of the Holy Spirit.

10. One of the worst things a church can do is to take men or women right out of prison or those who have recently completed a recovery

program and put them on "Front Street." This feeds their pride and self-centeredness. These are the roots of addiction. Addicts can be, and many are, gifted individuals, but they need to forget their gifts for a while and humble themselves (see 1 Timothy 3:6 and 1 Timothy 5:22).

Step Overview

Step 1: Admit – Step 1 is to be viewed from the perspective of an unsaved individual. This is a picture of a person who has finally come to the realization that there is a God. Helpful verses to emphasize this condition would be:

The fear of the Lord is the beginning of knowledge (Proverbs 1:7). Knowing there is a God and that God will hold you accountable is the beginning of knowledge/wisdom.

But without faith it is impossible to please him: for he that cometh to God must believe that he is. (Hebrews 11:6)

Step 2: Believe – This step is to be viewed in light of Step 1. A person in an unsaved condition has acknowledged that God does exist (Step 1). Now the decision must be made as to who that God is. The person is in a searching mode at this point. In Step 2, the unsaved person reaches an intellectual conclusion that Christ is God.

In the beginning was the Word, and the Word was with God, and the Word was God. (John 1:1)

And the Word was made flesh, and dwelt among us. (John 1:14)

Step 3: Decide – This is the most important of all the steps. This is going from intellectual knowledge (Step 2) to heart knowledge. In this step, there is a surrender of the will at the foot of the cross. We lay down our wills and receive God's will and direction. When we believe the gospel, we receive the Holy Spirit, who empowers us and enables us to have the strength to overcome our addiction. Step 3 is the salvation step.

Note: The gospel should be presented in every class. Where is the gospel to be found in the Bible? First Corinthians 15:3-4: *For I delivered unto you first of all that which I also received, how that Christ died for our sins according to the scriptures; and that he was buried, and that he rose again the third day according to the scriptures.* What must we believe in order to say, "The Lord is my Shepherd"? Answer: the gospel.

NOTES

_____

_____

_____

_____

_____

_____

_____

_____

_____

_____

_____

_____

_____

_____

_____

_____

_____

_____

_____

For I am not ashamed of the gospel of Christ: for it is the power of God unto salvation to everyone that believeth. (Romans 1:16)

Neither is there salvation in any other: for there is none other name under heaven given among men, whereby we must be saved. (Acts 4:12)

Ye are of God, little children, and have overcome them: because greater is he that is in you, than he that is in the world. (1 John 4:4)

Step 4: Search – This is like looking for strengths and weaknesses of the other team as you are watching the game film when preparing for a football game. In this case, we are our own opposition. We are looking for strengths and weaknesses in ourselves. "I have met the enemy and he is me."

Weaknesses: Look for signs of pride and self-centeredness (not in other people, but in ourselves). These roots of addiction are a good place in which to start our inventory.

Strengths: We all have gifts, and we need to identify these gifts and develop them in the way God has intended for us to use them.

Our inventory must be true and honest. Bad information gathered here will result in a defective plan in Step 5.

But have renounced the hidden things of dishonesty, not walking in craftiness, nor handling the word of God deceitfully; but by manifestation of the truth commending ourselves to every man's conscience in the sight of God. (2 Corinthians 4:2)

If we say that we have no sin, we deceive ourselves, and the truth is not in us. (1 John 1:8)

Step 5: Acknowledge – We are going on the offense. We are going to formulate a game plan and put it into practice. Keep it real. "No dope is better than bum dope." We need to recognize our own brand of kryptonite. It will weaken and destroy us. It will diminish us to the extent that we will look nothing like the person God created us to be. We need to get away from it or get it away from us. We are made in the image of God, the Creator of all things; therefore, we tend to create what we imagine. If we can imagine a life lived free from addiction, then we can create that life.

But be ye doers of the word, and not hearers only, deceiving your own selves. (James 1:22)

God is a Spirit, and they that worship him must worship him in spirit and in truth. (John 4:24)

I can do all things through Christ which strengtheneth me. (Philippians 4:13)

With men this is impossible; but with God all things are possible. (Matthew 19:26b)

Step 6: Change – The key to Step 6 is the word *willing*. Is the addict ready to do whatever is necessary to be set free from his or her addiction? There is no turning back. The extent to which we are willing to change is directly proportional to the amount of change that will take place. Also, we must allow God to do the changing. Many times we give up control of our lives (surrender) only to take control again when we feel better physically and become more self-confident. We need to guard against this.

I protest by your rejoicing which I have in Christ Jesus our Lord, I die daily. (1 Corinthians 15:31)

And Jesus said unto him, No man, having put his hand to the plough, and looking back, is fit for the kingdom of God. (Luke 9:62)

So then because thou art lukewarm, and neither cold nor hot, I will spue thee out of my mouth. (Revelation 3:16)

Step 7: Ask – The key word in this step is *humbly*. By not trying to draw on our own power to enact change, we turn instead to God, drawing on the power (dunamis in Greek which means dynamite) we receive from the Holy Spirit. We acknowledge that we cannot change ourselves, but only God can change us. We also acknowledge our need to change and our own inability to do so if left to our own devices. We acknowledge that we are flawed beings and sinners in need of being rescued from ourselves. We need a clear view of who we are and who God is; this understanding will lead to humility. Only God can forgive sin.

The fear of the Lord is the instruction of wisdom; and before honour is humility. (Proverbs 15:33)

Before destruction the heart of man is haughty, and before honour is humility. (Proverbs 18:12)

By humility and the fear of the Lord are riches, and honour, and life. (Proverbs 22:4)

NOTES

And Jesus said unto him, Why callest thou me good? There is none good but one, that is, God. (Mark 10:18)

Note: What Jesus is saying in Mark 10:18 is, "You are right in calling Me good, but do you really understand that you are right?"

Step 8: Restore – This step is often used by the enemy to put us under conviction. Under conviction, we are less effective in our Christian walk and witness. There are many obstacles to making complete restitution. We cannot possibly know the extent of the harm we have caused others. Sin has a ripple effect, so we trust in God to give us the desires of our hearts, trusting that He will let us know what He wants us to do. He will give us the *want-to*s. We are not to minimize the need for restitution, but we need to be aware of the difficulties involved. First and foremost, we need to walk in God's forgiveness.

Delight thyself also in the Lord: and he shall give thee the desires of thine heart. (Psalm 37:4)

If the wicked restore the pledge, give again that he had robbed, walk in the statutes of life, without committing iniquity; he shall surely live, he shall not die. (Ezekiel 33:15)

I have seen his ways, and will heal him: I will lead him also, and restore comforts unto him and to his mourners. (Isaiah 57:18)

Step 9: Pursue – This step answers the question, "Now that I am saved, how shall I live?" Life is an ongoing process, and this step should also be an ongoing process. God's will for us is to have a personal relationship with His Son. God's plan for our lives is to share that relationship. God's purpose is to glorify Himself.

The Lord is not slack concerning his promise, as some men count slackness, but is longsuffering to us-ward, not willing that any should perish, but that all should come to repentance. (2 Peter 3:9)

But sanctify the Lord God in your hearts: and be ready always to give an answer to every man that asketh you a reason of the hope that is in you with meekness and fear. (1 Peter 3:15)

And he said unto them, Go ye into the world, and preach the gospel to every creature. (Mark 16:15)

Let your light so shine before men, that they may see your good works, and glorify your Father which is in heaven. (Matthew 5:16)

Step 1

Admit

I admit that my life is not my own and is beyond my ability to manage or control. I have become powerless over the substance or substances that I have abused. I acknowledge my need for God to set me free from all the things in this world that have me ensnared and prevent me from being the person God created me to be.

(Discuss each Bible verse by asking, "How does this particular verse apply to Step 1?")

Note: This step brings us to the end of ourselves. We admit to ourselves that no matter how hard we try, we just cannot get it right. We are, in fact, committing a form of self-inflicted destruction and are unable to stop. No matter how hard we try to swim against the current, we are being swept along into the abyss. Part of us wants to grab on to something, anything that will make it stop; but another part of us wants to continue even if it means destroying everything we love or care about, even if it means destroying ourselves. The part that wants to continue our destructive habits seems the stronger of the two.

O Lord, I know that the way of man is not in himself: it is not in man that walketh to direct his steps. (Jeremiah 10:23)

Man's goings are of the Lord; how can a man then understand his own way? (Proverbs 20:24)

Note: A man cannot direct his steps. God never intended us to take on this world by ourselves. He always intended it to be a partnership. The best sentence an addict can utter is, "I can't." It is important to understand that our lives are not our own. This changes our perspective from being self-centered to being God-centered.

The earth is the LORD's, and the fullness thereof; the world, and they that dwell therein. (Psalm 24:1)

Thine, O Lord, is the greatness, and the power, and the glory, and the victory, and the majesty: for all that is in the heaven and in the earth is thine; thine is the kingdom, O Lord, and thou art exalted as head above all. Both riches and honour come of thee, and

NOTES

_thou reignest over all; and in thine hand is power and might; and
in thine hand it is to make great, and to give strength unto all._
(1 Chronicles 29:11-12)

_For the invisible things of him from the creation of the world are
clearly seen, being understood by the things that are made, even
his eternal power and Godhead; so that they are without excuse._
(Romans 1:20)

Q. How would pride and self-centeredness prevent us from taking this first step?

_For my thoughts are not your thoughts, neither are your ways my
ways, saith the Lord._ (Isaiah 55:8)

Note: God's ways are not our ways. In fact, God's ways are usually the opposite
of ours. The world teaches us that as addicts, we have low self-esteem; the truth
is that we are full of pride. The world teaches that we need to build ourselves
up; the truth is that all we think about is ourselves. _The two primary roots to
any addiction are pride and self-centeredness._

Pride

Definition: A high or inordinate opinion of one's own dignity, importance,
merit, or superiority, whether as cherished in the mind or as displayed in bear-
ing or conduct.

Synonyms: vainglory, high-minded, boastful.[1]

Note: The key to our definition of pride is the word _inordinate_: exceeding
reasonable limits or unreasonableness based in falsehood.[2]

_Why should ye be stricken anymore? Ye will revolt more and more:
the whole head is sick, and the whole heart faint. From the sole of
the foot even unto the head there is no soundness in it; but wounds,
and bruises, and putrifying sores: they have not been closed, neither
bound up, neither mollified with ointment._ (Isaiah 1:5-6)

Q. These verses may be used to describe the life and mindset of an addict. Can
you identify with these verses? (Discuss)

_How art thou fallen from heaven, O Lucifer, son of the morning!
How art thou cut down to the ground, which didst weaken the
nations! For thou hast said in thine heart, I will ascend into heaven,
I will exalt my throne above the stars of God: I will sit also upon the
mount of the congregation, in the sides of the north: I will ascend
above the heights of the clouds; I will be like the most High. Yet thou_

---

1   _http://www.dictionary.com/browse/pride?s=t._
2   _http://www.thefreedictionary.com/inordinate._

shalt be brought down to hell, to the sides of the pit. They that see thee shall narrowly look upon thee, and consider thee, saying, Is this the man that made the earth to tremble, that did shake kingdoms; that made the world as a wilderness, and destroyed the cities thereof; that opened not the house of his prisoners? (Isaiah 14:12-17)

Q. What was the devil's sin?

A. Pride

List the "I wills" of Lucifer in your notes.

Why do the heathen rage, and the people imagine a vain thing? The kings of the earth set themselves, and the rulers take counsel together, against the LORD, and against his anointed, saying, Let us break their bands asunder, and cast away their cords from us. He that sitteth in the heavens shall laugh: the LORD shall have them in derision. (Psalm 2:1-4)

Q. What does vain mean?

Q. What do you think the vain things were that the people imagined?

And the whole earth was of one language, and of one speech. And it came to pass, as they journeyed from the east, that they found a plain in the land of Shinar; and they dwelt there. And they said one to another, Go to, let us make brick, and burn them thoroughly. And they had brick for stone, and slime had they for morter. And they said, Go to, let us build us a city and a tower, whose top may reach unto heaven; and let us make us a name, lest we be scattered abroad upon the face of the whole earth. And the LORD came down to see the city and the tower, which the children of men builded. And the LORD said, Behold, the people is one, and they have all one language; and this they begin to do: and now nothing will be restrained from them, which they have imagined to do. Go to, let us go down, and there confound their language, that they may not understand one another's speech. So the LORD scattered them abroad from thence upon the face of all the earth: and they left off to build the city. Therefore is the name of it called Babel; because the LORD did there confound the language of all the earth: and from thence did the LORD scatter them abroad upon the face of all the earth. (Genesis 11:1-9)

Discuss: The tower of Babel.

Q. Why have men always sought to be their own gods?

NOTES

A. Pride

Q. Do you think you can get to heaven on your own merits?

Q. Have you tried to do things your way? What was the result?

> *Though the LORD be high, yet hath he respect unto the lowly: but the proud he knoweth afar off.* (Psalm 138:6)

> *And whosoever shall exalt himself shall be abased; and he that shall humble himself shall be exalted.* (Matthew 23:12)

> *But he giveth more grace. Wherefore he saith, God resisteth the proud, but giveth grace unto the humble.* (James 4:6)

Note: An acronym we can use is GRACE: God's Riches At Christ's Expense.

Q. How would you define grace?

Q. Who is the receiver of God's grace?

> *For thus saith the high and lofty One that inhabiteth eternity, whose name is Holy; I dwell in the high and holy place, with him also that is of a contrite and humble spirit, to revive the spirit of the humble, and to revive the heart of the contrite ones.* (Isaiah 57:15)

> *The LORD is nigh unto them that are of a broken heart; and saveth such as be of a contrite spirit.* (Psalm 34:18)

> *The sacrifices of God are a broken spirit: a broken and a contrite heart, O God, thou wilt not despise.* (Psalm 57:17)

Note: Having a humble heart allows me to draw nearer to God. *Contrite* or *contrition* comes from the primary root word for powder. A heart that has been crushed into powder is a heart that God can truly use. Do you want to be used by God? Humble yourself.

Q. How do we overcome our pride?

A. By seeing ourselves honestly and squarely the way God sees us. This should lead to repentance, which could lead to salvation. (Discuss)

Self-centeredness

Definition: Concerned solely or chiefly with one's own interests, welfare, etc., engrossed in self; selfish; egotistical. Independent, self-sufficient; centered on oneself or itself. Archaic; fixed; unchanging.[3]

Synonyms: egocentric, selfish, know-it-all, stuck on oneself.[4]

Now the works of the flesh are manifest, which are these; adultery, fornication, uncleanness, lasciviousness, Idolatry, witchcraft, hatred, variance, emulations, wrath, strife, seditions, heresies, Envyings, murders, drunkenness, revellings, and such like: of the which I tell you before, as I have also told you in time past, that they which do such things shall not inherit the kingdom of God. But the fruit of the Spirit is love, joy, peace, longsuffering, gentleness, goodness, faith, Meekness, temperance: against such there is no law. (Galatians 5:19-23)

Read and study Galatians 5:19-23. On the left side list the works of the flesh, and then on the right side list the fruit of the Spirit.

Q. On which side of the ledger would you prefer to live?

Q. In the above verses, what are the differences between works and fruit? (Discuss)

A. Works are self-produced, under the law, and lead to death. Fruit is Spirit-produced, not under the law, and leads to life.

Know ye not that the unrighteous shall not inherit the kingdom of God? Be not deceived: neither fornicators, nor idolaters, nor adulterers, nor effeminate, nor abusers of themselves with mankind, nor thieves, nor covetous, nor drunkards, nor revilers, nor extortioners, shall inherit the kingdom of God. (1 Corinthians 6:9-10)

Flesh defined: Our sinful nature which we have received as the result of the original sin of Adam.

Note: Sin came into the world through one man.

Wherefore, as by one man sin entered into the world, and death by sin; and so death passed upon all men, for that all have sinned. (Romans 5:12)

Sin defined: Doing something God told us not to do (this is a sin of commission); not doing something God told us to do (this is a sin of omission). Sin is disobedience to God.

Discuss: The fall and the depravity of man as found in Genesis 3.

---

3   *http://www.dictionary.com/browse/self-centered?s=t.*
4   *http://www.thesaurus.com/browse/self-centered?s=t.*

NOTES

So God created man in his own image, in the image of God created he him; male and female created he them. (Genesis 1:27)

This is called the creation theory or intelligent design.

Q. What is the world's answer to this verse?

A. Darwinism/evolution

For all have sinned, and come short of the glory of God. (Romans 3:23)

Discuss: For all have sinned and fallen short of the glory of God.

As it is written, There is none righteous, no, not one. (Romans 3:10)

But the scripture hath concluded all under sin, that the promise by faith of Jesus Christ might be given to them that believe. (Galatians 3:22)

For the wages of sin is death; but the gift of God is eternal life through Jesus Christ our Lord. (Romans 6:23)

Discuss: The wages of sin is death.

That as sin hath reigned unto death, even so might grace reign through righteousness unto eternal life by Jesus Christ our Lord. (Romans 5:21)

The sting of death is sin. (1 Corinthians 15:56a)

Then when lust hath conceived, it bringeth forth sin: and sin, when it is finished, bringeth forth death. (James 1:15)

Wherefore, as by one man sin entered into the world, and death by sin; and so death passed upon all men, for that all have sinned. (Romans 5:12)

Discuss: So death passed upon all men.

Q. Why am I responsible for Adam's sin? (Discuss)

Note: Adam had the "power of attorney" for all mankind. Do you think that if you had been Adam, the outcome would have been better? Adam would have been held responsible for Eve's sin even if he had not eaten of the forbidden fruit, because he, as the head of the family, would have been held accountable.

Sin is like using a credit card. It is fun to use for a little while, until you get the bill. It never tells you the cost up front. It feeds on your pride; all you have to do is sign your name. It can affect what you do in the future. It can put you in bondage. It can restrict you from doing things you want to do. It can damage your family and relationships.

Discuss: Sin puts us in bondage.

Q. What is the result of giving in to my sinful nature (flesh)?

A. You have aligned yourself with the enemies of God.

> *Ye are of your father the devil, and the lusts of your father ye will do. He was a murderer from the beginning, and abode not in the truth, because there is no truth in him. When he speaketh a lie, he speaketh of his own: for he is a liar, and the father of it.* (John 8:44)

> *For all that is in the world, the lust of the flesh, and the lust of the eyes, and the pride of life, is not of the Father, but is of the world.* (1 John 2:16)

Q. How do we overcome self-centeredness?

A. By seeing the needs of others before our own.

Q. How do we begin to see the needs of others?

A. By praying for others.

Note: When we pray for others, we are acknowledging a power greater than our own; therefore, we are taking ourselves out of the center. When we pray for others, we begin to see their needs and then we begin to want to meet those needs. When we begin to meet the needs of others, we begin to sacrifice our own wants for the needs of other people. This is what the Bible means by living your life as a living sacrifice (Romans 12:1). You are never going to have life until you begin to give it away.

NOTES	Works of the Flesh With Definition	Fruit of the Spirit With Definition
_____	_____	_____
_____	_____	_____
_____	_____	_____
_____	_____	_____
_____	_____	_____
_____	_____	_____
_____	_____	_____
_____	_____	_____
_____	_____	_____
_____	_____	_____
_____	_____	_____
_____	_____	_____
_____	_____	_____
_____	_____	_____

Need some help? See Addendum "Breaking it Down," B-1 through B-6.

On which side of this ledger do you choose to live? The answer should be a no-brainer, yet if we are honest with ourselves, we choose the left side over the right, time and time again.

Founder's Notes with Illustrations for Step 1

> **Step 1 – Admit:** I admit that my life is not my own and is beyond my ability to manage or control. I have become powerless over the substance or substances that I have abused. I acknowledge my need for God to set me free from all the things in this world that have me ensnared and prevent me from being the person God created me to be.

Founder's Note 1, Step 1:

The first part of Step 1 is referred to by addicts as reaching rock bottom. The problem is that what many perceive to be rock bottom is just a series of rock bottoms along the way. Addicts must come to the end of themselves. They must be at a point where the only option left is to choose to surrender. I am not talking about taking a time-out from addiction, which is what many do when they go into rehab or even into prison. In their minds, they are buying more time in order to put themselves in a position to start up again. They may even use the fact that they have been to rehab or have been rehabilitated as a means to regain people's trust in order to use and abuse those same people again. Addicts are users and abusers of people, and they will do so over and over again until they are compelled to see the reality and magnitude of their depravity.

I was so depraved that I stole from my kids' piggy banks, always with the false promise that I would pay them back. I never did. What the addict needs to realize and what is emphasized in Step 1 is the need to be at the end of the rope. There are no more time-outs. You cannot continue. You are done. The picture here is of someone who is blindfolded and walking the plank on a pirate ship. The person is at the end of the plank; one more step and it is off to oblivion. There is no turning to the left or to the right; there is no turning back.

A question I ask at this juncture is, "How much hell are you willing to put yourself, your family, and others through before you say, 'That's enough'?" I remember being on my knees in my prison cell, confessing to God that I had hurt a lot of people, begging Him not to let me hurt anyone else. I pleaded with Him to just take me home if I was ever going to hurt someone again.

Ask them: Are you through hurting others? Are you through hurting yourselves? Do you understand that your thinking is flawed? Do you see your need to change?

If an addict does not see the need to change, there will be no change.

Founder's Note 2, Step 1:

Many times I have heard inmates say, "God put me here for a reason," or "The devil made me do it." The truth is that God did not put them there. James 1:13 says, *Let no man say when he is tempted, I am tempted of God: for God cannot be tempted with evil, neither tempteth he any man.* God will use inmates where they are, but God did not put them there, nor did the devil make them do it. The devil hates us because we are made in God's image. The devil wants us dead. He wants us destroyed. John 10:10 says, *The thief cometh not, but for to steal, and to kill, and to destroy.* Satan certainly does not want us studying God's Word, wherever we may be. So who put these inmates in prison? They did!

I was working in a juvenile center when a young girl told me that her father was in prison and that she always had been told she would be like her father. "So here I am," she said, "in prison just like my dad." I asked her if she knew that the actions she had taken that resulted in her being sentenced to the juvenile center were wrong. She said, "Yes, I knew I was doing wrong." Next I asked her when she would begin to start taking responsibility for her own choices and actions. I wanted her to take responsibility for what she did. I wanted her to see that her actions put her before a judge and resulted in her being sentenced to a juvenile facility. There comes a time in each of our lives when we must take responsibility for our own choices. Implicit in Step 1 is the need to take responsibility for one's own actions. Addicts need to understand that they are the primary cause of their condition. An addict needs to be able to say truthfully, "I have met the enemy and he is me."

Founder's Note 3, Step 1:

Following are two examples about substances and substances abused. The first example is that of Superman. Baby Superman was placed into a rocket by his parents and launched into outer space just seconds before the planet Krypton (where he was born) exploded. The rocket traveled through space and eventually crashed on earth, where Superman was raised by earthly parents. As Superman grew, it became obvious that he possessed superhuman qualities. The point I want to make is that Superman had one weakness, and that was being exposed to kryptonite, a piece of the very place where he was born. When exposed to kryptonite, Superman had to get away from it; if not, he would weaken and lose his superhuman powers. If exposed to kryptonite long enough, he would die.

As addicts, we all have our own kryptonite – things that are part of our world that seek to destroy us. First it weakens us, turning us into someone we never thought we would be, and then it seeks to destroy us. Whatever our kryptonite is, we need to get away from it or get it away from us. Although the substance or substances may vary from addict to addict, the roots of our addiction(s) remain the same. These roots are pride and self-centeredness.

The second example I use is when I was at a juvenile center in Ohio doing a Bible study about the story of Jacob. I was teaching from Genesis 25:29-34 about how Jacob had tricked his older brother, Esau, out of his inheritance (birthright) for a bowl of soup (pottage). As we were discussing the story, one young man raised his hand and asked in an incredulous tone, "How could Esau be so stupid as to give up his inheritance for a bowl of soup?"

My reply to the teen was, "You've been given an inheritance, too. How could you give that up for drugs?"

Founder's Note 4, Step 1:

To acknowledge a need for God is to acknowledge that there is someone greater than yourself. This is a big step in the life of an addict. The two best words an addict can utter are, "I can't." This then begs the question, "Who can?" Knowing that there is a God presents addicts with the concept of being accountable to that God, and it also presents them with the dilemma that their actions have deeply offended God. *The fear of the LORD is the beginning of wisdom* (Psalm 111:10).

In his book *Mere Christianity*, C. S. Lewis describes his coming to faith. First, he realized that there is a God. Next, he recognized that God is holy. Then, he understood that because God is holy, He must punish sin. Lewis recognized himself as a sinner. Truly this is the beginning of wisdom.

Founder's Note 5, Step 1:

Pride and self-centeredness are the two roots of any addiction. This should be repeated by statement and in question form again and again during the course of any meeting.

How do we overcome pride? By seeing ourselves honestly and squarely the way God sees us.

How does God see us? God sees us as sinners in need of a Savior.

How do we overcome self-centeredness? We overcome self-centeredness by seeing the needs of others before our own.

What is a good way to begin this process? We can begin by praying for others.

What do we know about roots? They need to be pulled out in order for whatever is being sustained by the roots to be destroyed.

For example, you cannot just cut off a weed at the top, or it will grow back. You need to pull out the weed along with its roots to eradicate it. In this case, the weed(s) represents our addiction(s), and the roots we want to pull out or eliminate are pride and self-centeredness. We know some roots grow deeper than others and are harder to pull out. Change is not going to be easy. Pulling out roots, like the dentist pulling out a tooth, can be painful. An addict must truly desire these roots to be removed, or the effort will fall short of the desired effect of a life free of addiction. It is easy to see pride and self-centeredness in others; the trick is to see them in ourselves.

People making comments should always be encouraged to include themselves in the comments. Sometimes in my classes someone points out what others need to be doing. After class, I always take that person aside and encourage him to include himself in his remarks. Saying "we" is always preferable to saying "you" when giving an example.

NOTES

NOTES

_____

_____

_____

_____

_____

_____

_____

_____

_____

_____

_____

_____

_____

_____

_____

_____

_____

_____

_____

Founder's Note 6, Step 1:

Early in my Christian walk, I decided to believe the Bible until I believed the Bible. I was led to this decision by a story I had read about the great Methodist minister, John Wesley. Wesley had been returning to England from the colonies when his ship was caught in a storm so severe that it threatened the ship and the lives of those on board. Wesley cowered and feared for his life, while the Moravian missionaries who were on the same ship sang hymns and lifted up praises to God. Once safely on land, Wesley understood that there was something lacking in his faith. He knew Jesus Christ intellectually, but not personally. Wesley determined never to preach again. However, Peter Böhler, a Moravian and Wesley's confidant, appealed to Wesley, imploring him not to give up preaching but instead to preach faith until he received faith. Wesley followed Böhler's advice and soon received faith when he was converted at a meeting on Aldersgate Street in London. The rest, as they say, is history.

In the past, I had often tried to read the Bible as an intellectual exercise, and I never got past the genealogies in the book of Genesis. However, after being born again, the Bible took on a whole new meaning to me. I knew it was God's Word and therefore true. I determined to believe it until I believed it. I also decided that if I read something that my intellect could not receive, I would pray the prayer a father in the New Testament prayed: *Lord I believe; help thou mine unbelief.*

I again read the account of woman being made from the rib of man, and I believed. I read how Noah built the ark, and I read about the flood, and I believed. I read about Moses parting the sea, and I believed. However, when I got to the book of Numbers, where there was a donkey that talked, I prayed, "Lord I believe; help thou mine unbelief." Pray for discernment and you will receive it. It came to me that I had heard many two-legged donkeys speak, and if the Lord who created all things wanted a donkey to talk, He could certainly get that done. I was now walking, hearing, and reading by faith. God's Word rang true. Concerning the tower of Babel, one might ask how God could take seriously the plans of men to build a tower into the heavens, but look at us today. We are exploring outer space. We are reaching into the heavens. If that had been the main focus of all mankind throughout history, it is very probable we would be going places today that we could never have imagined. God's Word is as true today as it was in the day of Babel.

Founder's Note 7, Step 1:

When discussing and defining sin, I find the credit card example to be most effective. Another effective tool is to draw a circle on a dry-erase board and say, "This is the perfect geometric shape. It has no beginning and no end. This is how God created us to be. However, sin has disfigured us and eroded us away (*slowly begin to erase the circle until it is gone*) to the point where we don't look anything like God created us to be."

Step 2

Believe

I believe that the God I need to restore my life and make me whole is to be found in the person of Jesus Christ, the Word who was with God, who is God, and who became flesh and dwelt among us.

(Discuss each Bible verse by asking, "How does this particular verse apply to Step 2?")

Note: During the period known as the Age of Enlightenment, the French writer Voltaire wrote, "If God did not exist, it would be necessary to invent him." What Voltaire meant was since the masses had no hope in this world but to serve the aristocracy, it would be necessary for those in control to keep the masses placated by giving them a make-believe hope in the next world. Although this statement was made by an atheist who was trying to explain the existence of God in a skeptical way, it really reinforces Christianity. Think about it. If you were to make up a god, would you make your god a carpenter who died on the cross? (Discuss)

Q. What does restore mean?

A. To bring back into existence or use; to bring back to an original or former desirable condition.[5]

Q. As addicts, do we need to be restored?

Note: Review Romans 3:23 and 6:23.

Can a man take fire in his bosom, and his clothes not be burned? (Proverbs 6:27)

Q. Does sin come with a cost?

Q. Do you know the cost up front?

Q. Will you ever know the entire cost of your sin and all the lives impacted by it?

---

5   http://www.dictionary.com/browse/restore?s=t.

Review Galatians 5:19-21:

Now the works of the flesh are manifest, which are these; adultery, fornication, uncleanness, lasciviousness, idolatry, witchcraft, hatred, variance, emulations, wrath, strife, seditions, heresies, envyings, murders, drunkenness, revellings, and such like: of the which I tell you before, as I have also told you in time past, that they which do such things shall not inherit the kingdom of God.

Q. Can you identify with any of these?

Q. How many of these works of the flesh do you think are rooted in pride and self-centeredness?

O wretched man that I am! who shall deliver me from the body of this death? (Romans 7:24)

Note: To be restored, we first need to be reconciled with God.

Q. What does reconciled mean?

A. To be restored to unity and peace.

Q. To whom should I turn for reconciliation and restoration?

Note: Millions and millions of people down through the generations have named the name of Christ, and their lives have been radically changed for the better! What does this say to you?

Q. Do you want to be delivered?

And almost all things are by the law purged with blood; and without shedding of blood is no remission. (Hebrews 9:22)

Q. What is the definition of purged?

Q. What is the definition of remission?

Q. What do you think was so special about the blood of Jesus? Discuss what this means to you.

But God commendeth his love toward us, in that, while we were yet sinners, Christ died for us. (Romans 5:8)

Note: We tend to try to be someone we are not because we are afraid that if people really knew who we are and what we think, they would not have anything to do with us. However, God knows every evil thought you have ever had or will have. He knows every sinful thing you have done or will do, yet He died for you anyway. God is saying, "Come to Me as you are and allow Me to do the changing."

Q. Why do you think God would die for you?

Q. Why was it necessary for God to die for you?

> *For if by one man's offence death reigned by one; much more they which receive abundance of grace and of the gift of righteousness shall reign in life by one, Jesus Christ.* (Romans 5:17)

Note: Death came into this world by the actions of one man, Adam. Life is restored back to us by one man, Jesus. Review the definition of grace.

> *And ye shall know the truth, and the truth shall make you free.* (John 8:32)

Q. What do you think the truth is that is being referred to in this verse?

> *I am the way, the truth, and the life: no man cometh unto the Father, but by me.* (John 14:6)

> *If the Son therefore shall make you free, ye shall be free indeed.* (John 8:36)

Q. How does the Son make you free?

> *Know ye not, that to whom ye yield yourselves servants to obey, his servants ye are to whom ye obey; whether of sin unto death, or of obedience unto righteousness? But God be thanked, that ye were the servants of sin, but ye have obeyed from the heart that form of doctrine which was delivered you. Being then made free from sin, ye became the servants of righteousness.* (Romans 6:16-18)

Q. How would you define righteousness?

Q. How do we become righteous?

> *But of him are ye in Christ Jesus, who of God is made unto us wisdom, and righteousness, and sanctification, and redemption.* (1 Corinthians 1:30)

NOTES

Knowing this, that our old man is crucified with him, that the body of sin might be destroyed, that henceforth we should not serve sin. (Romans 6:6)

Note: The first part of this verse is referring to the substitutionary death of Jesus.

Q. How does the death of Christ apply to the living?

Therefore if any man be in Christ, he is a new creature: old things are passed away; behold, all things are become new. (2 Corinthians 5:17)

Q. What does this verse mean to you?

Q. What do you think is meant by all things?

Note: C. S. Lewis wrote in his book *The Great Divorce* that the Christian life begins to blend into heaven the moment one accepts Christ. (Discuss)

Q. Do you want to be a new creature? Do you desire to be free from the things of the past?

For I am not ashamed of the gospel of Christ: for it is the power of God unto salvation to everyone that believeth. (Romans 1:16)

Q. What must I believe to be saved?

A. The gospel

For I delivered unto you first of all that which I also received, how that Christ died for our sins according to the scriptures; and that he was buried, and that he rose again the third day according to the scriptures. (1 Corinthians 15:3-4)

Note: The above verse is the gospel in a nutshell.

Q. What does the gospel mean?

Q. What is so good about Good Friday? After all, is not that the day Christ was crucified?

Q. What do you think Paul meant when he wrote, I delivered unto you first of all that which I also received?

Note: Read and discuss 1 Corinthians 15:3-22.

Jesus answered and said unto him, Verily, Verily, I say unto thee, Except a man be born again, he cannot see the kingdom of God. (John 3:3)

Note: We are all born physically alive but spiritually dead. To be spiritually dead implies a life void of and separated from God. The first birth would be the physical birth; without the first birth, the second would not be necessary. For those who are living, the second birth is as imperative as the first, if we are to see the kingdom of God.

For all have sinned, and come short of the glory of God. (Romans 3:23)

For the wages of sin is death; but the gift of God is eternal life through Jesus Christ our Lord. (Romans 6:23)

But God commendeth his love toward us, in that, while we were yet sinners, Christ died for us. (Romans 5:8)

That if thou shalt confess with thy mouth the Lord Jesus, and shalt believe in thine heart that God hath raised him from the dead, thou shall be saved. (Romans 10:9)

For whosoever shall call upon the name of the Lord shall be saved. (Romans 10:13)

Discuss: The Roman Road to Salvation.

Therefore being justified by faith, we have peace with God through our Lord Jesus Christ. (Romans 5:1)

There is therefore now no condemnation to them which are in Christ Jesus, who walk not after the flesh, but after the Spirit. (Romans 8:1)

For I am persuaded, that neither death, nor life, nor angels, nor principalities, nor powers, nor things present, nor things to come, nor height, nor depth, nor any other creature shall be able to separate us from the love of God, which is in Christ Jesus our Lord. (Romans 8:38-39)

But put ye on the Lord Jesus Christ, and make not provision for the flesh, to fulfill the lusts thereof. (Romans 13:14)

Discuss: The results of salvation found in the book of Romans.

NOTES

Note: Notice the order here: we must first put on Christ and then make no provision for the flesh. (Discuss)

Q. What do you think it means to put on the Lord Jesus Christ?

> For he saith, I have heard thee in a time accepted, and in the day of salvation have I succoured thee: behold, now is the accepted time; behold, now is the day of salvation. (2 Corinthians 6:2)

Q. If you have not already put on Jesus Christ, are you ready to receive the Lord Jesus Christ as your Savior?

Founder's Notes with Illustrations for Step 2

Step 2 – <u>Belief</u>: I believe that the God I need to restore my life and make me whole is to be found in the person of Jesus Christ, the Word who was with God, who is God, and who became flesh and dwelt among us.

Founder's Note 1, Step 2:

In Step 1, we came to the decision that there is a God. Now it is imperative that we get the right one! Why not Allah or Buddha or a host of other gods professed by those in the world? The answer lies in our basic tenet: the Bible is the Word of God, and God's Word is true. If a person will acknowledge that basic tenet, then we will be able to lead that person to the Lord. Once a person is confronted with the truth, then it is incumbent upon that person to receive the truth or turn away from the truth. This is an individual decision.

Founder's Note 2, Step 2:

On page 23 I wrote about Voltaire and how his cynical quote caused me to consider how a carpenter on a cross could be the one and only true God. There are other things that stood out to me as I began to study the Bible. In ages past, people worshipped the sun and the moon. Today we know that the sun is a star and the moon is a natural satellite of the earth. We know they are not gods. Genesis does not refer to the sun and moon as gods but as lights. The sun is to light the day and the moon is to light the night. We know this to be true. When I studied geology, I studied the water cycle; that cycle can be found in Isaiah 55. The Bible is a spiritual book and is not intended to be a science or geology book, but these things that I have mentioned above reinforced within me the truth of God's Word.

Founder's Note 3, Step 2:

When I was in prison and after being born again, I loved to study the Bible.

I noticed another inmate, a practicing Buddhist, who also studied the Bible. However, his goal for studying the Bible was to disprove it. I would watch him in the library reading secular books that attacked the Bible. He read commentaries along with the Bible, and he wrote down things he thought to be ridiculous or contradictory. He did this for several years. He considered himself to be a scholar. One day I was studying in the library when this man sat down next to me. Out of the corner of my eye I saw him searching the Bible, going back and forth through the pages. Finally, in exasperation he looked over at me and asked, "Could you tell me where to find the story of Jonah and the whale?"

I replied, "You might try the book of Jonah." God's Word is for God's people. It confounds the wise.

Founder's Note 4, Step 2:

When I was an inmate, I attended a prison service in which the chaplain was speaking about religions in general. He said all religions have some value. They take you out of the center and they set boundaries. As addicts, we are self-centered and have long ago stepped over the boundaries established by society as the norm. Religion attempts to restore those boundaries and establish a power greater than ourselves as the center of the universe. The difference is that all other religions are about what we can do for God. Only Christianity is all about what God did for us. There is joy in Christianity. It is not about *do*, but it is about *done*. It stands to reason that I cannot do anything that would make a perfect God more perfect, so why would He ask me to? One of the attributes of God is autonomy; He does not need anything or anyone in order to exist. I could not save myself and I cannot do anything to make God a debtor to me. I could not go to God, so God had to come to me, and He did this in the person of Jesus Christ. This rings true to me. I can think of no other way by which mankind could be saved.

Founder's Note 5, Step 2:

Why do we blame God for things that men do? In *A Case for Christ*, Lee Strobel writes about an evangelist (Charles Templeton) who became an agnostic and humanist after seeing a picture of a dead baby in an Ethiopian woman's arms. Templeton said he would not serve a god who allowed that to happen. As I was thinking about this, I realized that God did not draw the boundaries of Ethiopia. When God created the world, there were plenty of things to eat and drink, but man in his greed has determined who is to eat and who is to starve. Sin came into the world through the actions of one man, and with sin came death. We should not charge God with the things men do. I found this illustration to be helpful for those who have experienced pain or loss, to get them to reconsider their view of God. I want them to see that God is love. It is true that the fear of God will put you on your knees, but it is the love of God that will keep you there in praise and thanksgiving.

NOTES

Founder's Note 6, Step 2:

I get a newsletter from Kovels, a company that deals in antiques and collectibles. I was surprised to read in one newsletter about a Superman comic book that sold for over two million dollars! That got me thinking about the blood of Christ. How much would one drop of Christ's blood be worth in today's market? The price would be beyond measure. Therefore, I must be of great value to God, because that blood has been applied to me. *And almost all things are by the law purged with blood; and without shedding of blood is no remission.* (Hebrews 9:22)

Founder's Note 7, Step 2:

Regarding the substitutionary death, Christ did not die for sinless sinners. You need to come as you are. It is great that He died for sinners. It is great that He died for others, but it means nothing if you cannot say that He died for you. You can say that the Lord is *a* shepherd or that He is *the* shepherd; but you must be able to say, "He is *my* shepherd." When teaching in prison, I use the example of a man sentenced to death, sitting in the electric chair, when another man offers to take his place. I ask, "What does the man in the chair need to do?"

The answer I am looking for is, "He needs to get out of the chair!"

"Some of you," I tell them, "are still in the chair. You need to get out before the switch is flipped, and you can't get out."

Founder's Note 8, Step 2:

Is it easier to sin or to serve Christ? Most addicts say it is easier to sin. Some Christians will even say it is easier to backslide than to be obedient. Why is that? It is because they have to give up pleasing the flesh. They actually feel like they are giving something up to become a Christian or to be obedient. They do not consider the cost, the total cost, of the lifestyle they are living. I will then ask them to imagine being at the end of their life in which they had continued in sin and contrast it to the end of their life if they had lived for the Lord. Which life do you think was easier?

Refer back to your Galatians 5:19-23 notes from page 15. Addicts do not count the cost. They tend to minimize or compartmentalize the cost and see it being paid off in some kind of installment plan. It does not work that way. Payment in full can be demanded at any time. As the saying goes, "Sin will take you farther than you want to go, keep you longer than you want to stay, and cost you more than you want to pay."

Founder's Note 9, Step 2:

The Son will set you free. This is what it means to be forgiven. In the old days, if you wanted to start your life over, you went west, took an assumed name, and started again. Today with computers, credit card tracking systems, etc., you cannot go west, but you can start over. You can be a new person. You can be forgiven. Isn't it great to be forgiven? To be free from the wages of sin and death and to be free to start over is a wonderful thing.

One day I was walking the prison yard with a Christian brother when he said to me, "Larry, if we really understood what Christ did for us on the cross, our joy would be so complete that this fence couldn't contain us. We would be doing backflips right now!"

When I'm teaching, I always ask, "Don't you want to be forgiven?" If there is no desire to be forgiven, then there is no desire to change. I tell the students that they do not have to go out like that; they can go out forgiven. I don't care what men call you or what labels society has assigned to you; if you know the Son as your Savior, you have been forgiven, and God calls you a friend. You will never get a better deal than that.

Founder's Note 10, Step 2:

Concerning 2 Corinthians 5:17: I was attending a mission conference in Mississippi when I heard the preacher say, "This verse is referring to the inner man; only the inside things become new."

My Bible doesn't say that. My Bible reads, *all things are become new* (2 Corinthians 5:17). Why do people always seek to put their own limits on this verse? The answer is that man forgives selectively, but God forgives completely. It seems like every denomination has an ax to grind or a bone to pick with this verse. Either God's Word is true and all things become new, or God is a liar and just some things become new.

I remember when I was born again. The way I looked at the world around me changed. I saw God's hand in His creation. I saw His beauty and His magnitude for the first time. The geese flying overhead, the blue sky, the trees, everything looked new to me. The way I looked at people was new. I saw them in the light of God's love, and I began to love them, too. For example, I have a cousin Billy whom I never liked. I think I was jealous of him because my dad often talked very favorably about him. Billy was a sheriff, and I think that had something to do with it as well. Cousin Billy was one of the first people I saw when I was released from prison. I remember looking out the window of my parents' home and seeing Billy coming up the driveway. I thought, "Lord, you are putting me to the test early!" However, Cousin Billy and his wife, Vaunda, were born again, and we had a great visit that day. Then it dawned on me that perhaps the reason I had not liked Billy in the past was because he was a Christian. What does darkness have in common with light? Today, I often hear from my cousin; he and his wife are very supportive of my ministry.

Does 2 Corinthians 5:17 mean that we will not have to face the consequences of our past behavior? While it is true that in God's eyes we are white as snow, we still must face our past. We will have problems carried over from past sins. However, the way we look at those problems, our desire to deal with those problems, and the problems themselves (which no longer look insurmountable) will become new! We no longer have to deal with those problems on our own. Our Lord will never leave us or forsake us. In Christ, we can do all things. We face our problems in the light of God's Word, and if God be for us, who can be against us? I am convinced that 2 Corinthians 5:17 means exactly what it says:

NOTES

*Therefore if any man be in Christ, he is a new creature: old things are passed away; behold, **all things are become new**.*

Founder's Note 11, Step 2:

I wrote earlier about being born physically alive but spiritually dead. To help explain this, we can compare ourselves to computers. Being physically alive, information is being downloaded to us through our five senses (sight, hearing, touch, smell, and taste). We then process this information, and we make decisions based upon what we have processed. For example, because of what I have learned from my senses, if I see a fire, I walk around it and not through it. This information is constantly being downloaded to us and processed by the brain, which results in decisions being made and action being taken or not taken. However, it is true that there are more things unseen than seen. For example, a simple chair has molecules holding it together. There are atoms with protons and neutrons. Gravity is holding that chair in place. I cannot see these things, but they exist. I cannot see a cold virus, but I know it exists. I cannot see the vast expanse of the universe, but I know it is out there. The bottom line is that nothing is as simple as it seems.

Every human being has a spiritual part, which is a connection that needs to be plugged in to the Spirit of God in order for us to understand things that exist in the spiritual realm. Once we get plugged in, the Holy Spirit starts downloading information and light that illuminates things that were previously in the dark. As a result, we have better and more complete information upon which to base our decisions. The more information we have, the better decisions we will be able to make, and the results of those decisions will be better, too. So how do we get spiritually plugged in? We get spiritually plugged in when we receive the Holy Spirit. This happens when we put our faith and trust in Jesus.

Decide

> I have decided to turn from the things of the past (repent) and to ask Jesus to be lord and manager of my life (surrender).

(Discuss each Bible verse by asking, "How does this particular verse apply to Step 3?")

Note: Unfortunately, many people never complete Step 2. They may even go as far as believing that Jesus is who He said He is, but this is only intellectual knowledge. They see, they believe, but they do not receive. They make the decision that Jesus and Christianity are not for them. There is no repentance. There is no surrender. At the foot of the cross, a transfer of the will must take place. We lay our will down and receive God's will, God's plan, and God's purpose for our lives. What we know to be true in our heads needs to be transferred to our hearts.

> *To open their eyes, and to turn them from darkness to light, and from the power of Satan unto God, that they may receive forgiveness of sins, and inheritance among them which are sanctified by faith that is in me.* (Acts 26:18)

Q. Who is me in the above verse?

Q. We do not just receive forgiveness of sins when we turn to Jesus; what else do we receive?

Q. What does an inheritance mean to you?

> *For if ye turn again unto the Lord, your brethren and your children shall find compassion before them that lead them captive, so that they shall come again into this land: for the Lord your God is gracious and merciful, and will not turn away his face from you, if ye return unto him.* (2 Chronicles 30:9)

Note: *For if ye turn again.* This could refer both to those who have backslidden and to those who are turning from death to life for the first time.

Q. When God blesses you, who else gets blessed?

NOTES

Q. How do we return unto Him?

A. If backslidden, confess and repent. If turning from death to life, through Christ.

Discuss the Parable of the Prodigal Son:

> *And he said, A certain man had two sons: And the younger of them said to his father, Father, give me the portion of goods that falleth to me. And he divided unto them his living. And not many days after the younger son gathered all together, and took his journey into a far country, and there wasted his substance with riotous living. And when he had spent all, there arose a mighty famine in that land; and he began to be in want. And he went and joined himself to a citizen of that country; and he sent him into his fields to feed swine. And he would fain have filled his belly with the husks that the swine did eat: and no man gave unto him. And when he came to himself, he said, How many hired servants of my father's have bread enough and to spare, and I perish with hunger! I will arise and go to my father, and will say unto him, Father, I have sinned against heaven, and before thee, And am no more worthy to be called thy son: make me as one of thy hired servants. And he arose, and came to his father. But when he was yet a great way off, his father saw him, and had compassion, and ran, and fell on his neck, and kissed him. And the son said unto him, Father, I have sinned against heaven, and in thy sight, and am no more worthy to be called thy son. But the father said to his servants, Bring forth the best robe, and put it on him; and put a ring on his hand, and shoes on his feet: And bring hither the fatted calf, and kill it; and let us eat, and be merry: For this my son was dead, and is alive again; he was lost, and is found. And they began to be merry. (Luke 15:11-24)*

Note: Review God's plan of salvation. Have you received Jesus? If you have received Jesus, you will change. You have entered into a partnership with God. That is good news! How fast you will change depends largely (not entirely) on the sincerity of your repentance and the extent of your surrender. God requires us to surrender unconditionally. However, we sometimes want to cut a deal with God. Christian growth is directly proportional to our dependence upon God. He will do His part, but what He does will also depend on what you allow Him to do. You may not notice it at first, but you will begin to change. The fact that you are changing will become more and more apparent to you. The exciting thing is that others will see it, too!

> *That ye put off concerning the former conversation the old man, which is corrupt according to the deceitful lusts; And be renewed in the spirit of your mind; And that ye put on the new man, which after God is created in righteousness and true holiness. (Ephesians 4:22-24)*

Note: This is a process we can only achieve when we receive God's new nature. Review 2 Corinthians 5:17. Remember that in this verse, *all things* means exactly that – *all things*. Do not let anyone deceive you and say some things are not under God's grace.

Q. How would you define the word conversation as used above?

A. A way of life (see Ephesians 4:19).

Q. What does it mean to be renewed in the spirit of your mind? Could this be a return to sanity?

Note: When you take something off, you must put something on. It is like filling the seats on a Ferris wheel. You do not fill them all at once, but you fill one seat at a time. As the Ferris wheel comes to a stop, people get off and new people get on. We need to unload the old habits and put on new habits, not all at once, but one habit or group of habits at a time.

Discuss Matthew 12:43-45:

> *When the unclean spirit is gone out of a man, he walketh through dry places, seeking rest, and findeth none. Then he saith, I will return into my house from whence I came out; and when he is come, he findeth it empty, swept, and garnished. Then goeth he, and taketh with himself seven other spirits more wicked than himself, and they enter in and dwell there: and the last state of that man is worse than the first. Even so shall it be also unto this wicked generation.*

Note: What happened when we tried to stop practicing our addiction(s) in the past? Didn't the desire to use return to us much stronger than before? It is not enough to sweep the house clean; we need to fill it up so when temptation knocks powerfully on our door again (and it will), we will be able to say, "Go away! This is no longer your house, and there is no room for you here."

Q. In what condition did the unclean spirit find his house when he returned to it?

Q. Did he return alone?

Q. Will he be harder to remove after this return? (Discuss)

> *Lie not one to another, seeing that ye have put off the old man with his deeds; and have put on the new man, which is renewed in knowledge after the image of him that created him.* (Colossians 3:9-10)

Note: One of the hardest things for an addict to give up is lying. We do it instinctively; it has become a way of life, and we are good at it. Learning to tell

NOTES

the truth takes practice and faith. The best way to practice telling the truth is to share it with other believers. We need to live in the truth. We need to embrace the truth about ourselves. We cannot do this without God's help.

Note: The word *deeds* in this verse is a picture of something that is ongoing, something that has been a practice. There will always be a battle between what our flesh (our sinful nature) wants to do and the renewal process that is taking place within us. (Discuss)

Q. Change for most of us is a slow process. Why do you think God does not just transform us immediately and be done with it?

> *If my people, which are called by my name, shall humble themselves, and pray, and seek my face, and turn from their wicked ways; then will I hear from heaven, and will forgive their sin, and will heal their land.* (2 Chronicles 7:14)

Note: This is one of the most frequently quoted verses in the Bible. Let us take a little time to study and discuss it.

Q. To whom is God talking?

Q. What are the four things God calls His people to do in the above verse?

Q. What does it mean to seek His face?

Q. How do we receive forgiveness? To whom is God talking? (Repeated for emphasis)

Q. What do you think God meant when He said, "I will heal their land"?

Note: What God does on a universal scale, He will do on an individual scale.

Q. Do you and your family need healing? What should you do?

> *But seek ye first the kingdom of God, and his righteousness; and all these things shall be added unto you.* (Matthew 6:33)

Note: As previously written, one of the goals of this program is to develop an attitude of gratitude toward God. A good way to begin this is to pray first thing in the morning, "God what would you have me do this day?" This simple prayer sets the tone for our day. We are not saying, "This is what I want to do or have to do this day." Instead, we are asking God to direct our steps, which enables us to enter into a far greater world than just self.

Q. How do we receive God's righteousness?

A. Review 1 Corinthians 1:30.

Q. What do all these things mean to you? (Discuss)

> *Remember ye not the former things, neither consider the things of old. Behold, I will do a new thing.* (Isaiah 43:18-19a)

Note: If all things become new, then we need to say goodbye to the past. "Yesterday is history, tomorrow is a mystery, and today is a gift. That's why we call it the present." We need to forgive the things and people who have hurt us in the past. If we do not forgive, we allow those things and people to continue to affect us in a negative way. We need to give those things and people to the Lord. We need to start life anew. Old friends who do not know Christ have nothing in common with you anymore. The Bible says that darkness has nothing in common with light. We are to be in the world, but not of the world. (Discuss)

> *If ye then be risen with Christ, seek those things which are above, where Christ sitteth on the right hand of God. Set your affection on things above, not on things on the earth. For ye are dead, and your life is hid with Christ in God. When Christ, who is our life, shall appear, then shall ye also appear with him in glory.* (Colossians 3:1-4)

Note: These verses describe our new life in Christ. His glory is now our glory, and His Father calls us His friend.

Founder's Notes with Illustrations for Step 3

Step 3 – Decide: I have decided to turn from the things of the past (repent) and to ask Jesus to be lord and manager of my life (surrender).

Founder's Note 1, Step 3:

This is the most important step in an individual's life; without this, everything else is just going through the motions. Without this decision, the power that enables us to live a life free from addiction is denied to us. Second Timothy 3:5 says, *Having a form of godliness, but denying the power thereof: from such turn away.* Conviction, repentance, and surrender are the keys that place us in a position to receive the Lord Jesus, who offers the gift of eternal life.

Founder's Note 2, Step 3:

Several years ago, I was invited to attend a prison service being held by an ex-inmate. He claimed to have led over 11,000 inmates to professions of faith

NOTES

during the past year through his ministry. At that point, I was not skeptical; I was impressed and curious as to how he conducted his services. I was hoping to see or hear something that might be beneficial to my own services.

Soon, however, it became apparent to me that the speaker, although he had a strong testimony, did not know the Bible. He made several misstatements, one of which was referring to Moses as an uneducated man. I might have overlooked this because of the power of the individual's testimony, but what was done later could not be overlooked. At the end of the service, all those who attended were asked to stand up; then they were led in reciting "The Sinner's Prayer," after which they were all told they were saved. This was followed by the laying on of hands by the members of the ministry team who were conducting this church service. I was asked to help in this laying on of hands, and when I refused, I was asked, "Why?"

I replied, "Where is the repentance?" It is my belief that one can repent and not be saved; however, one cannot be saved without repenting. It is a terrible thing to tell people that they are saved when in fact that is not the case. Numbers can be misleading.

Founder's Note 3, Step 3:

I mentioned earlier that some people never get past Step 2. They accept the premise that Jesus is who He said He is, but refuse to acknowledge that He is the only way to heaven. They think that all roads lead to heaven. They have become magnanimous with God's grace as if they were the dispensers of it. In truth, we have all sinned against a holy God. We have lived lives that have denied His existence. We have openly, flagrantly, and purposely rebelled against and disobeyed Him. We deserve death, but we are offered life through Christ Jesus. Isn't it just like us to complain that there is only one way to enter into heaven, when in fact we do not deserve any way at all?

Founder's Note 4, Step 3:

As Christians, we have our own vocabulary, and we get so adept in its usage that we think that everyone knows what we are talking about. I witnessed a juvenile facility chaplain fall into this trap while he was speaking to about thirty teens. He repeatedly used the word *grace* during his message. When he finished and it was my turn to speak, I inquired if anyone could define the word *grace* for me. No one could. So how in the world could the teens have gotten anything out of the chaplain's message? Those who are reading, hearing, and studying this material must be able to understand the words being used. *Sanctified, justified, hope, faith, grace,* and many other common Christian words need to be defined and explained in such a way that anyone hearing or reading them can grasp their meaning. Let us not complicate the gospel. Let's keep it simple. If you are doing this as a self-study, do not be afraid to use a Bible dictionary or even a regular dictionary to help you understand the meaning of words or concepts.

Founder's Note 5, Step 3:

During a lunch break at a state prison where I was holding classes, I began a conversation with a young Catholic nun who had been teaching in the room next to mine. During the course of our conversation, she mentioned that a lot of people are lost forever because their knowledge of Christ had not travelled the approximate eighteen inches from their head to their heart. To this I smiled and replied, "Are you sure you are not a Baptist, Sister?"

Founder's Note 6, Step 3:

In discussing the parable of the prodigal son, I always point out that the son had come to the end of himself. He had reached rock bottom. To the Jews, the pig is an unclean animal, and I can think of nothing more degrading to a Jewish person than to be forced to clean up after pigs. If the prodigal son did not actually say the two best words an addict can say ("I can't"), I am sure he was thinking them, which in turn led him to the belief that his father could. He came under conviction, humbled himself, saw himself for who he truly was, confessed his sin, and repented. As a result, he was restored to a right relationship with his father. I believe the salvation process works in this fashion and involves the three people personified in the Holy Trinity:

1. Father – *No man can come to me, except the Father which hath sent me draw him: and I will raise him up at the last day.* (John 6:44)

2. Holy Spirit – *And when he is come, he will reprove the world of sin, and of righteousness, and of judgment: of sin, because they believe not on me.* (John 16:8-9)

3. The Son – *Jesus saith unto him, I am the way, the truth, and the life: no man cometh unto the Father, but by me.* (John 14:6)

Salvation is God's business. The Holy Spirit convicts; the Father draws to the Son those who have been convicted, and the Son returns to the Father those who have been cleansed by His blood.

Founder's Note 7, Step 3:

In the first note section, I mentioned trying to cut a deal with God. I have heard inmates pray, "Lord, if you give my wife back to me, I will serve you the rest of my life," or "Lord, if you grant me that judicial release, I will never use drugs again!" I am sure we can all relate to this type of prayer; however, we first need to consider to whom we are praying. God is the Creator of all things; by Him all things were created, and without Him not a thing was created that was created. He is omniscient. He knows our hearts better than we do. Let us consider this account in Matthew 26:31-35a:

> *Then saith Jesus unto them, All ye shall be offended because of me this night: for it is written, I will smite the shepherd, and the sheep of the flock shall be scattered abroad. But after I am risen again, I*

will go before you into Galilee. Peter answered and said unto him, Though all men shall be offended because of thee, yet will I never be offended. Jesus said unto him, Verily I say unto thee, That this night, before the cock crow, thou shalt deny me thrice. Peter said unto him, Though I should die with thee, yet will I not deny thee.

I am sure Peter meant it when he said he would never deny the Lord. I am sure he believed it at the time, but Jesus knew his heart. God is not looking to cut a deal with us. God is looking for our total, absolute, and unconditional surrender.

Founder's Note 8, Step 3:

In 2 Chronicles 7:14, God is talking to His people. God's people are flawed. God would not tell us to humble ourselves if we were already humble. The opposite of humility is pride. Pride is one of the roots of addiction. Many times in the Bible, God tells us to humble ourselves. I made the decision once to pray for humility. I asked God to humble me. The experience was not pleasant. It is better to humble ourselves than to have God humble us; take my word for it. You will be glad you did.

God goes on to say, "If my people . . . shall . . . pray"; therefore, we must not be praying. This is probably due to our self-centeredness, which is the other root of addiction. We are to seek His presence, His audience, and His approval. Instead, too many times we are like children whose mother has told them, "Wait until your father gets home!" We are avoiding God. We do not want to see Him because we are practicing sins that need to be confessed. We need to repent. We do not witness as we should because we know in our hearts that to do so would be hypocritical. We need to turn from our wicked ways, because continuing in sin inhibits us from praying, from witnessing, and from being a source of light in the world. Sin has covered up and dulled our light as a lampshade does a lamp. Christ died to set us free from sin. I pray that we will not get entangled in sin again, but if we do, let us confess our sins and turn away from them so we can be all we can be for Jesus.

Founder's Note 9, Step 3:

In Matthew 6:33 Jesus said, *But seek ye first the kingdom of God, and his righteousness; and all these things shall be added unto you.* I again stress Isaiah 55 where God tells us emphatically that His ways are not our ways. We tend to want to reverse the process found in Matthew 6:33. We tell God that if He does this or does that, then we will seek His kingdom. God's desire is to have us seek first His kingdom (a place where all is in perfect obedience to Him) and His righteousness. Then and only then will all these things be given to us. Please note that the righteousness of God is found in the person of Jesus Christ. Matthew 6:33 should be understood in the context of our receiving Christ.

Step 4

Search

I have made an honest search and moral inventory of myself, seeking to eliminate that which is not in accord with God's will for my life.

(Discuss each Bible verse by asking, "How does this particular verse apply to Step 4?")

But be ye doers of the word, and not hearers only, deceiving your own selves. (James 1:22)

Note: We should always read the Bible with the goal of applying what we read to our daily lives. If we are serious about change, it would be useful for us to have a plan of action. In order to have a plan of action, we must first gather some information about ourselves upon which we can act. The plan will be different for each individual, because the list that will be developed from this search will be unique to each individual. While the cycle of addiction is the same for all addicts, it is also true that we all have different triggers and our very own kryptonite. (Discuss)

The addiction itself is not the problem but is a manifestation of the problem (or problems) that we must begin to deal with here in Step 4. Why are we the way we are? How did we get to where we are? These are tough questions, and there are no shortcuts we can take to find the answers. We need to be painstakingly thorough in our search if we want this step to work for us. Step 4 is an information gathering step in which we get a good look at the old self and are introduced to the new self.

Q. So how do we begin this honest search and moral inventory?

A. We start with what we know to be true, and we build upon it.

Let's review:

Q. What are the two primary roots of addiction?

A. Pride and self-centeredness

Q. How do we overcome pride?

41

NOTES

A. We overcome pride by seeing ourselves honestly and squarely the way God sees us. (Discuss)

Note: Keeping it real with ourselves and with God is the key to Step 4. Real information results in a real plan of action.

Q. Our honest search and moral inventory also requires us to be fearless. The word fearless is a peculiar but fitting way to describe how we need to approach the process of taking our own unique and individual inventory. What would this fearless approach have to do with keeping it real or seeing ourselves honestly?

Q. Can taking an inventory be painful to the one taking it?

Note: While walking the prison yard one morning, I happened to glance up to see the sun glistening off the razor wire. I realized that even with the sun reflecting off it, there was still nothing pretty about razor wire. Suddenly another thought hit me like a cement truck. That razor wire was not designed to give off an artistic glow from the sun. That razor wire was there to keep me inside this fence! I was so bad that they had to put razor wire at the top of the fence to keep me in! The fence was not built to keep people from getting to me but to keep me from getting to people! Until then if you had asked me if I was a nice guy, I would have answered, "Yes," even though I had three different prison numbers! It is easy to deceive ourselves.

Q. Can we deceive ourselves while taking an inventory? Give some examples. (Discuss)

Q. How do we overcome self-centeredness?

A. By seeing the needs of others before our own. (Discuss)

Note: If we know that the two primary roots of addiction are pride and self-centeredness, then it would make sense to begin our personal inventories by searching for signs of these roots in our lives. Roots need to be pulled out completely if we are to destroy that which is being produced and sustained. This can be a very painful process. Reality is a painful business, yet God is calling us to embrace the life He has given each of us and to worship Him in spirit and in truth.

Create in me a clean heart, O God; and renew a right spirit within me. (Psalm 51:10)

Note: Reciting this verse from Psalm 51, which was written by David after he had committed some terrible sins, is certainly a good way to begin taking an inventory. The only change that matters and the only change that is lasting starts from within. Isaiah 55:8 tells us that God's ways are not our ways. In fact, God's ways are often the exact opposite of our ways. The world seeks to change us from the outside in, but God seeks to change us from the inside out.

Q. Which way (inward or outward) do you think change is more effective? (Discuss)

Q. What do you think David meant by a right spirit?

Q. How would a right spirit help us as we go about the process of taking a personal inventory?

Q. Who does the changing?

> *Search me, O God, and know my heart: try me, and know my thoughts: and see if there be any wicked way in me, and lead me in the way everlasting.* (Psalm 139:23-24)

Note: Any personal inventory needs to start with God doing the searching. The psalmist who wrote the above verses is not saying, "I'm going to do" but instead is asking God to "Help me do." We need to acknowledge that God has a better view of our spiritual condition than we do. Many times, sin hides itself from the sinner, and many times we tend to give ourselves a pass when we should not. Notice that there is an implied willingness expressed by the psalmist to submit to any change that God would deem necessary. He is also willing to take action, but only in partnership with God.

Q. Discuss some methods God could use to search our hearts.

Q. What did the psalmist mean when he asked God to try him?

Q. What do you think the way everlasting is?

> *I the Lord search the heart, I try the reins, even to give every man according to his ways, and according to the fruit of his doings.* (Jeremiah 17:10)

Note: In this verse, God says that He will *try the reins*. He will give every man *according to his ways* and *according to the fruits of his doings*. This is equivalent to the biblical principle of reaping what you sow. As we do our personal inventory, it is important that we look for habits that lead to planting bad seeds. It is also important that we look for those habits which lead to planting good seeds. We need to search out both the good and the bad within ourselves, seeking to eliminate the bad and doing our best to reinforce that which is good.

NOTES

Q. What does try the reins mean to you?

Q. What is the best way for a man to go if he desires God's provision?

Let's review:
Contrast the works of the flesh (sinful nature) with the fruit of the Spirit (see Galatians 5:19-23). (Discuss)

Q. Which would you rather reap?

Note: Fruit can either be bad or good. It all depends on who is doing the producing. If the flesh is the producer, then the fruit will be bad, resulting with us breaking the law and eventually dying. If the fruit is produced by the Spirit of God, then there is no law against it. You can have as much of this fruit as you like, and it does not hurt you or others. It leads to life.

> Take heed unto thyself, and unto the doctrine; continue in them: for
> in doing this thou shalt both save thyself, and them that hear thee.
> (1 Timothy 4:16)

Note: There is a saying that misery loves company. Sin likes company, too. A drunk is quick to offer someone a drink, because drinking with someone else is viewed as more fun than drinking alone. The same is true of drug addicts and sex addicts; they are always looking to draw others in. That is the problem when someone says, "Whatever happens between consenting adults behind closed doors is their business." Sin never stays behind closed doors. It is always looking for new recruits.

Our actions in the past have influenced others in negative ways. (Discuss)

However, now the reverse can be true; our actions can actually influence people in positive ways. We were once on the road that leads to death, but now we are on the road that leads to life. We can set an example for others that may lead them to life. We need to be painstakingly thorough with our inventory. It really is a matter of life and death.

> Be ye followers of me, even as I also am of Christ. (1 Corinthians 11:1)

Note: Our goal in taking an inventory is to come up with a plan that would enable us to make the above statement.

> God forbid: yea, let God be true, but every man a liar; as it is writ-
> ten, That thou mightest be justified in thy sayings, and mightest over-
> come when thou art judged. (Romans 3:4)

Note: While taking our inventory, we may become confused. The world may say it is right and legal to do certain things, yet you know that God's Word clearly states that it is not. As Christians, we are to obey the law of the land; but what if that law contradicts the law of God? Acts 4:18-19 tells us that Peter and John were faced with just such a dilemma; they were ordered by the authorities *not to speak at all nor teach in the name of Jesus,* implying that the punishment would be severe if they did. Yet Peter and John answered, *Whether it be right in the sight of God to hearken unto you more than unto God, judge ye.* God's Word is true, and we need to hold all things up to the light of God's Word. God, not man, is the ultimate judge of what is right and wrong.

Q. What does it mean to be justified in thy sayings? Look up the definition of justified, and discuss it in the light of this verse.

Q. How do we come out on the right side of things when we are judged?

> *And he said unto them, Ye are they which justify yourselves before men; but God knoweth your hearts: for that which is highly esteemed among men is abomination in the sight of God.* (Luke 16:15)

Note: The goal of our inventory is not to please men, but to please God.

Q. What does esteemed mean? What does abomination mean? Give some examples of what men esteem that would be offensive in the sight of God.

Note: What we hold on to and what we let go of needs to line up with God's Word.

Founder's Notes with Illustrations for Step 4

Step 4 – <u>Search</u>: I have made an honest search and moral inventory of myself, seeking to eliminate that which is not in accord with God's will for my life.

Founder's Note 1, Step 4:

A good plan requires good information. When I played high school football, we would watch game films and look for the weaknesses and strengths of the team we were going to play. From that information, we would formulate a game plan. This is the way I approach Step 4. However, the game film that I am looking at here is all about me. I am looking at my weaknesses and my strengths, and from that information I am going to formulate a game plan that will result in a life set free from addiction.

Ask them, "How would you define *honest*?"

We define honest as truthful; honorable in principles, intentions, and actions.[6]

---

6   *http://www.dictionary.com/browse/honest?s=t.*

Founder's Note 2, Step 4:

It matters what you are thinking. It matters what the intent is behind your actions. For example, opening the door for a lady may be a chivalrous act or an indecent act, depending on the true intent behind the action. Before we begin our inventory, we must come to grips with why we are doing our inventory. Are we just going through the motions? Are we just buying time until we are in a position to use again? Are we trying to please ourselves and others, or are we trying to please God? These are some of the questions we need to resolve before we begin our inventory. What would be some other questions that we may need to resolve before we begin Step 4?

Founder's Note 3, Step 4:

We can take different approaches to being honest. For example, imagine that we are at the beach and I ask the person next to me to hold my wallet, which contains two hundred dollars, while I go for a swim. I think anyone would agree that the person holding my wallet was dishonest if, while I was swimming, he had taken off with it. I think we would also agree that the person was honest, if upon my return from swimming, he handed my wallet to me with the money still inside.

There is another scenario, though. What if I had held out my wallet for the person to hold and he had said to me, "Please don't give me that; it's just too much of a temptation for me"? I would think that person was honest, as well. The result would be the same as with the honest man who had returned my wallet to me. I would still have my wallet with the two hundred dollars inside. The last person, though, acknowledged his weakness. Somewhere in the past he had taken an honest self-inventory. What would prevent a person from admitting such a weakness? The answer is pride. An addict must do away with pride. An addict needs to be able to say to others, "I can't do that."

Once after I shared the above example in a prison class, an inmate in his early thirties approached me and asked if he could talk to me about a serious matter. This inmate was married and had two daughters. He was also labeled as a sexual offender because of the crime for which he was serving time. After serving several years, he had gone to his parole hearing and had been granted parole. His wife agreed to take him back. This meant that he had somewhere to be paroled to, which is important for a sex offender. I know of many sex offenders who, upon receiving a parole, cannot be released because they have no place to go. There are very few halfway houses for sex offenders.

This man was fortunate because he was going home. However, what he told me that day shook me to my core and cemented within in me forever the knowledge of the power of God's Word. The inmate made this simple statement: "After hearing you today, I came to the realization that I need to be honest with myself and with my family. When I left home, my daughters were very young, just babies really, and now they are in their teens. After all these years in prison, I am afraid I might be a threat to them. What do I do?" I asked him what he felt he should do, and he said he thought he should be honest. He then asked me if I would help him do that. This man knew he was risking his parole, his marriage, and everything he held dear, but he had determined to do the right thing. As a result, I suggested he talk with his case manager, who in turn called his wife, who called her pastor. They set up a visit in which some ground rules were established. His daughters were informed of the rules. He was allowed to go home, and his relationship with his wife and family is now one of love, honor, and respect. God is good.

Founder's Note 4, Step 4:

The famous seventeenth-century French philosopher, René Descartes, wrote a famous line in his "Discourse of Method" that is still often quoted today. He wrote, "Cogito ergo sum" or "I think, therefore I am." The thought here is that to doubt one's existence is to prove one's existence. Taking this idea logically, we can come to the conclusion that if thinking is proof of one's existence, then what we think must be important. The truth is that what we think defines the kind of person we are. The Bible speaks often to us about vain imaginations. Vain imaginations are useless thoughts which have no value and are without any lasting significance or importance. As addicts, we need to take control of our imaginations. Why? Because we are made in the image of our Creator, and we tend to create that which we imagine. We can choose to imagine and plan good things, or we can choose to imagine and plan destructive things, destroying the very things and individuals that we love.

Founder's Note 5, Step 4:

Addiction is just a manifestation of a bigger problem, or in many instances, bigger problems. Sin is progressive. The cycle of sin starts with a thought that is contradictory to the will of God. If that thought is not immediately dismissed but we choose to entertain that thought, then it becomes sin.

The next step we take is the rehearsal. We begin to fantasize what it would be like to act out the thought. For most people, there are barriers (perceived consequences) that keep them in check right here. For example, they are afraid they might get caught, might get divorced, or might shame or lose their family. They may even go to prison. Drugs and alcohol short-circuit the barrier process. It is equivalent to pouring gasoline on a building that is already aflame. We tend not to care if we get caught, or we minimize the consequences of getting caught. I would actually drink so that I would be able to act out. I had one inmate tell me that he would make a conscious decision to get high in order to get up the courage to rob a bank.

Founder's Note 6, Step 4:

Moral is defined in the *American Heritage College Dictionary* as "Of or concerned with the judgment of the goodness or badness of human action or character; conforming to standards of what is right or just in behavior; ethical." It is important to put the emphasis on the Word of God as our authority and the standard by which we judge that which is moral.

NOTES

In Nazi Germany during the 1930s and 1940s, eliminating the Jewish population and confiscating their property was viewed by those in authority as right; therefore, laws were passed making this legal. When these same authorities were tried for war crimes in Nuremburg, the judge who sentenced them was of another opinion. The judge said there is a law that takes precedence over the laws of men, and that is the law of God. He said that in God's eyes, every life on earth has meaning and value. The Nazis had violated this law and had put themselves in the position of deciding who was to live and who was to die. Only God has the right to do that.

When we do our moral inventory, we must hold it up to the truth of God's Word. I really don't care what man defines as sin. I do care what God defines as sin. Today, we are calling many things right that God's Word calls wrong. Today, just as it did in Nazi Germany, the truth will prevail. God's Word is true, and if you compromise the truth or distort it in order to fit a different standard (perhaps a standard embraced by a majority of the people), then the truth becomes something other than the truth.

Founder's Note 7, Step 4:

When taking our inventory, we must not minimize our faults or attempt to excuse them. Society will give us every reason to fail. There are many people in our nation who seek to reinforce failure while resenting and debasing those who are successful (I mean this as God defines success).

Here is an example from a sermon that I listened to while in prison. In this sermon, Pastor Knute Larson said, or perhaps quoted, "Those who seek the truth will be mocked. Those who find the truth will be isolated. Those who speak the truth will be killed so that others can go on living a lie in peace." Matthew Henry wrote, "The Word of God irritates the carnal mind."

The world seeks to change people from the outside in. You will be told that you have failed because you have grown up in a dysfunctional home. What you will not be told is that many people who have grown up in dysfunctional homes or even orphanages have gone on to lead good and productive lives. You will be told that you have failed because of the poor neighborhood in which you grew up. Yet a not-so-insignificant number of people who grow up in good neighborhoods, myself included, become addicts and criminals, while others who grow up in poorer neighborhoods succeed in life and become small business owners, teachers, statesmen, and more. Could it be all about your education level? This is not the case, either. Highly educated people have committed some pretty heinous crimes. Highly educated people become addicts. I have concluded that honest, hardworking people, regardless of their level of education, live happier and more complete lives.

Perhaps you have been told that you have failed because you were unable to find work. Yet, I know many men and women who have been released from prison, get a good job, and still end up back in prison. That leaves us with genetics. Some say that we have flawed genes or we were born that way, and as a result, we are permanently disabled. Out of all the excuses offered to us by the world, I believe this to be the saddest. A genetically flawed person is beyond hope, but alcoholics can and do recover – they are not without hope. If we call sin what it is, then we have an opportunity to overcome that sin and be healed. If we call sin what it is, then we can accept what Christ did for us on the cross, and we can be forgiven. We have this hope.

My grandfather on my father's side was an alcoholic. My father was an alcoholic. My oldest brother, Chuck, died from alcohol abuse. My brother Richard was close to losing his mind because of alcohol abuse. My sister was an addict. In some cases the children tend to bow down to the same idols their parent or parents worshipped. That is the generational curse. One could say it is genetic, but I say it is a choice.

I choose Jesus as my Lord and Savior, and today I choose not to drink. God changed me from the inside out. Herein lies the solution. If you put a person with an evil heart in a newer neighborhood, you have upgraded his victim list. You have given him a raise. If you educate a person with an evil heart, you have an educated evil person. If you give an evil person a job, that person does not cease to be evil. The only way that change makes sense is to first change the person's heart and then help that person get an education. That will result in the person getting a better job, which in turn will result in the person living in a better neighborhood or even improving his current neighborhood.

So, how do we change a person's heart? We cannot, but God can; that is what this program is all about. *Seek ye first the kingdom of God and his righteousness, and all these things shall be added unto you* (Matthew 6:33).

Founder's Note 8, Step 4:

I will return to Isaiah 55:8 and restate how God has told us in His Word that His ways are not our ways. In fact, many times our ways are the exact opposite of God's ways. This verse is a good case in point. We want to reverse the order here. We say to God, "You do this and give us this and then we will serve you." We might want to know everything up front first before we respond to God. God may tell us to go to such and such a place, and we ask, "Why?" God may not show us why until we get there.

I remember the first time the Lord called me to Alabama. At that time, I was just starting out in the ministry. I didn't know anybody in Alabama, and I did not have the funds to get there. So, being human, I questioned God's rationality and argued that I had more than enough ministry to do in Ohio. God then took me in His Word to Jeremiah 1:1-7. I can paraphrase the way it was applied to me as, "Don't argue. Don't give Me any excuses. Just do as I tell you and testify of Me." Trust was the key. I left for Alabama with a gas card and six dollars in my pocket. The result was that the ministry of Changed Lives and I were blessed beyond measure. Seeking God's kingdom will lead to God directing your life. Seeking God's kingdom will help you see the things within you that God desires to change. As you seek God's kingdom, you will learn step by step to depend on Him for all your needs. Keep this verse in its proper order and *all these things shall be added unto you.*

NOTES

Founder's Note 9, Step 4:

When we do our honest search and moral inventory, we are seeking to untangle ourselves from those things that have ensnared us in the past.

In facilitating this program, I always ask what some signs of pride would be in our day-to-day walk. A major sign is how many arguments or disagreements we get into during the course of a day. How easily angered are we? I point out that there are people who will deliberately try to antagonize you. They will try to elicit a certain negative response from you, and by doing so, they will control you. I ask, "Are you willing to allow someone to be wrong?" It is sad to think that the only time some people read the Bible is when they are trying to prove another person wrong.

A good biblical example (we should always be looking for biblical examples) can be found in 1 Corinthians 8:4-13, where Paul discusses meat sacrificed to idols and false gods. To paraphrase Paul, as mature Christians we know that these idols and false gods do not exist, so it is all right to eat this meat, but an immature Christian may think otherwise. If we do something that we truly think is a sin when in reality it is not, we are still actually sinning.

Paul goes on to say that instead of allowing a weaker brother to sin in such a manner by eating the meat offered to idols, he would rather refrain from eating the meat. To put it another way, Paul did not slap this weaker brother on his head with a biblical scroll and tell him to grow up! Instead, Paul demonstrated patience towards this individual, allowing this person time to grow in the Lord.

I was talking with a prison chaplain one day about how to measure a person's Christian growth. The chaplain said we should never assume that we are more mature than someone else just because we know more of the Bible than they do. He went on to say, "You don't know how many dragons that person had to slay just to get to where he is."

Founder's Note 10, Step 4:

Spotting signs of self-centeredness could be as easy as asking, "When was the last time I prayed for another person?" Praying for others leads us to see the needs of others, which in turn prompts a desire within us to meet those needs. This usually requires our time, our money, or both. In the process, we become willing to sacrifice something we desire in order to meet the needs of someone else. Another good question to ask is, "How much stuff do I really need?" I am amazed when I watch *American Pickers* on television and see how attached people are to the stuff they have accumulated over the years. They actually have an emotional attachment to these things. They are addicted to hoarding worldly things. We are not to love things; instead, we are to love people. Addicts use people and love things. God wants us to use things and love people.

Step 5

Acknowledge

Before God, others, and myself, I acknowledge my inventory to be true. I now begin to use the information from my inventory, formulating a plan that will result in a life set free from addiction.

(Discuss each Bible verse by asking, "How does this particular verse apply to Step 5?")

Note: We have compiled our inventory, looking especially for signs of pride and self-centeredness. These are the primary roots of addiction, and they need to be removed if we are to have a life free of addiction. We have acknowledged our weaknesses and our strengths. We have asked God to forgive us our sins, and we trust that He has cast them as far away as the east is from the west. We are a new creation, being conformed to the image of God. Now we get to work. It is time to get in the game. It is time to keep it real. As someone once said, "I have met the enemy and he is me." Now we can engage the foe. In Step 5, we go on the offensive.

Q. At this point, do we have a complete self-inventory?

A. No, but we should have a good start.

Q. Will it ever be completed?

A. No. (Discuss)

Note: Let's take a moment to talk about how the Bible is constructed. This is a classroom exercise and is not meant to be connected to the following verses (see addendum Basic Bible Exercise, page 130).

The Christian has three enemies: the flesh, Satan, and the world. We need to recognize our enemies and study their ways. The enemy will always come at us where he has beaten us before.

Q. Of the three, which do we have most control over? Discuss the percentages.

A. The flesh – 70%. The world – 15%. Satan – 15%.

NOTES

Q. What do we mean by the flesh?

A. Our sinful nature

I thank God through Jesus Christ our Lord. So then with the mind
I myself serve the law of God; but with the flesh the law of sin.
(Romans 7:25)

Q. Life is about choices, and choices have consequences. What are the two choices laid out here?

For they that are after the flesh do mind the things of the flesh; but
they that are after the Spirit the things of the Spirit. (Romans 8:5)

Q. What do you think it means to be after the flesh? Give some personal examples of being after the flesh.

Q. How can we be after the Spirit? (Read Psalm 37:1-8 and discuss.)

Q. What are the two choices we have in these verses?

Note: It is time to review and discuss Galatians 5:16-26. In verse 26 we read about envying one another. This has to do with comparing what we have with what someone else has and then envying the other person. It seems we never compare ourselves to those who have less; instead, we always compare ourselves to those who have more.

Q. Why do we make comparisons?

Q. Do you think comparing what we have with what someone else has is a good thing or a bad thing?

Q. Making comparisons leads to coveting. What does it mean to covet?

A. To desire another's property wrongfully.

For to be carnally minded is death; but to be spiritually minded is life
and peace. (Romans 8:6)

Q. What does carnally mean? What does incarnate mean? Discuss the difference.

Q. Life is about choices. What are the two choices presented in Romans 8:6?

Q. How does having choices line up with predestination?

So then they that are in the flesh cannot please God. (Romans 8:8)

But without faith it is impossible to please him: for he that cometh to God must believe that he is, and that he is a rewarder of them that diligently seek him. (Hebrews 11:6)

Q. Who cannot please God?

Q. In what do you think being in the flesh is rooted?

Q. What do we know about pride and self-centeredness?

Q. According to Hebrews 11:6, what pleases God?

Q. What are the choices the above verses present to us?

Q. What choices have you made in the past and how did those choices work out? Did the outcome agree with what is written in the Bible? (Discuss)

Q. If you had to choose today to please God or to displease God, which would you choose?

Note: The good news is, if Christ died for you (I use the word *if* because you must be born again to receive the Spirit of God), the conversion process that is taking place in you (you are being conformed to the image of God's Son) will empower you to have victory over addiction. You do not have to go out of this world an addict; you do not even have to go another day. That is good news!

But ye are not in the flesh, but in the Spirit, if so be that the Spirit of God dwell in you. Now if any man have not the Spirit of Christ, he is none of his. (Romans 8:9)

Whosoever shall confess that Jesus is the Son of God, God dwelleth in him, and he in God. (1 John 4:15)

Q. How do we receive the Spirit of God?

Q. Are the Spirit of God and the Spirit of Christ the same?

The Spirit itself beareth witness with our spirit, that we are the children of God. (Romans 8:16)

Hereby know we that we dwell in him, and he in us, because he hath given us of his Spirit. (1 John 4:13)

NOTES

And because ye are sons, God hath sent forth the Spirit of his Son into your hearts, crying, Abba, Father. (Galatians 4:6)

According to the above verses:

Q. Can we know beyond any doubt that we have received the Spirit of God?

Q. If we have the Spirit of God, are we saved?

Q. Is it possible to know beyond any doubt that we are saved?

And this is the record, that God hath given to us eternal life, and this life is in his Son. He that hath the Son hath life; and he that hath not the Son of God hath not life. These things have I written unto you that believe on the name of the Son of God; that ye may know that ye have eternal life, and that ye may believe on the name of the Son of God. (1 John 5:11-13)

Wherefore thou art no more a servant, but a son; and if a son, then an heir of God through Christ. (Galatians 4:7)

Note: You will never be offered a better deal than this. It just doesn't get any better than being an heir of God through Christ. This is your new identity in Christ. This is who God intended you to be all along. You can hold your head up, not because of who you are but because of who you are in Him. Jesus is the lifter of heads. Our shame has been cast aside, and His glory is now our glory. (Discuss)

And that he died for all, that they which live should not henceforth live unto themselves, but unto him which died for them, and rose again. (2 Corinthians 5:15)

I beseech you therefore, brethren, by the mercies of God, that ye present your bodies a living sacrifice, holy, acceptable unto God, which is your reasonable service. (Romans 12:1)

Note: This verse has often been used incorrectly as some kind of a "do penance" verse because of how some translate what it means to be a *living sacrifice*. How do we measure our lives? We measure our lives in time (seconds, minutes, hours, days, months, years). We are the only created thing that has attempted to measure time. How would we understand God's gift of eternal life if we had no concept of time? When we lay our will aside to serve others, we are giving of our time, and therefore we are laying down our life for the sake of others. Jesus said, *Greater love hath no man than this, that a man lay down his life for his friends* (John 15:13). Jesus laid down His life for us, so out of gratitude, we lay down our lives for others. We become living sacrifices, and this is our reasonable service. This is the proper response to the love Christ demonstrated to us on the cross.

> *Therefore, brethren, we are debtors, not to the flesh, to live after the flesh.* (Romans 8:12)

Note: We do not owe our enemies anything. We have been duped, deceived, and nearly destroyed by the enemies of God. Sin put us in debt and made us slaves to our enemies, but the blood of Christ set us free, and it is to Him we are indebted.

> *Submit yourselves therefore to God. Resist the devil, and he will flee from you.* (James 4:7)

Note: If we lay down our will and do the things God has called us to do, we will resist the devil's bidding, and he will have no choice but to move on; but, he will be back, and next time he will come back better prepared and stronger. You also will need to be prepared and strong.

Q. How can we prepare ourselves to resist the devil, the flesh, and the world?

> *There hath no temptation taken you but such as is common to man: but God is faithful, who will not suffer you to be tempted above that ye are able; but will with the temptation also make a way to escape, that ye may be able to bear it.* (1 Corinthians 10:13)

Note: Here is another often misunderstood verse in the Bible. It is often paraphrased incorrectly as, "God will not give us more than we can handle." This verse is clearly talking about temptation. The word used here for temptation can also mean trial. Temptation is a trial. When we are tempted, we are being tried. Will we do what is right in God's eyes, or will we do what is right in the eyes of the world and pleasing to the flesh? We will not be tempted beyond that which we can overcome. God will provide a way out, if we are looking for a way out. That is the key: we need to be looking for the way out and not the way in.

> *I speak after the manner of men because of the infirmity of your flesh: for as ye have yielded your members servants to uncleanness and to iniquity unto iniquity; even so now yield your members servants to righteousness unto holiness.* (Romans 6:19)

Note: Paul is calling on us to serve Christ with all the zeal that we had when we chased after our addictions. Our desire to change must be stronger than our desire to give in to the flesh. We also need a burning desire to live a life

NOTES

that is free from addictions, and we need the confidence to know that victory is assured in Christ.

Q. What does yield mean?

A. It means to give over to. This is not just surrendering; it is totally selling out.

Q. Do we have a choice as to whom or to what we yield?

Q. Notice the term unto holiness. What does that mean to you?

Sanctify yourselves therefore, and be ye holy: for I am the Lord your God. (Leviticus 20:7)

Q. What does sanctify mean?

A. To purify or free from sin. To consecrate or set apart for a purpose.[7]

Because it is written, Be ye holy; for I am holy. (1 Peter 1:16)

Q. What does holy mean?

A. Spiritually pure.

There is therefore now no condemnation to them which are in Christ Jesus, who walk not after the flesh, but after the Spirit. (Romans 8:1)

Q. Is it possible for us to be holy?

Q. How do we obtain holiness?

And be not conformed to this world: but be ye transformed by the renewing of your mind, that ye may prove what is that good, and acceptable, and perfect, will of God. (Romans 12:2)

Note: The Bible refers to *vain imaginations* many times. Vain means worthless or useless. As addicts, we use our imaginations as a hiding place to avoid responsibility and as a defense mechanism to avoid the pain of reality. We use our imaginations as a comfort zone in which to conceive sin. It becomes a warm fuzzy den of iniquity to which we cannot wait to retreat. We like being there and we go there every chance we get. The problem with that is we are made in the image of God the Creator, and we tend to create that which we imagine. Therefore, we need to change those things we imagine that produce negative results into those things we imagine that result in us doing things in a positive

---

7   http://www.dictionary.com/browse/sanctify?s=t.

way. If we imagine good things, we will plan good things, and good things will happen.

Q. Is there a constant pressure being applied to us to conform to this world? Name some ways we are conformed to this world.

Q. How do you think our minds are renewed?

Note: The second part of this verse is misused many times. God's perfect will does not need to be proven by us. God's Word is true. When the Pharisees told Jesus that His testimony was not true because He bore record of Himself, Jesus said to them, *Though I bear record of myself, yet my record is true* (John 8:14). Why? Because He didn't need to prove anything; He was the proof and the embodiment of all things true. However, God's will is proven by the lives we live and the thoughts we think. Our deeds will prove that this is the purposeful life God intends for all those who would seek Him and come to know Him. Our changed lives are lives that are good and acceptable and the result of God's perfect will being lived out in us and through us.

> *These things I have spoken unto you, that in me ye might have peace. In the world ye shall have tribulation: but be of good cheer; I have overcome the world.* (John 16:33)

Q. Does being a Christian mean all your troubles are over?

Q. Are you still going to have to deal with things from your past?

Q. What will be the difference between the life you lived in the past and the life you live today as a Christian?

Note: Christianity offers us many things. Peace is something we never experienced as addicts, but we now have peace and hope; in the past, there was no hope for us, but only despair.

> *But if the Spirit of him that raised up Jesus from the dead dwell in you, he that raised up Christ from the dead shall also quicken your mortal bodies by his Spirit that dwelleth in you.* (Romans 8:11)

Q. Review 1 Corinthians 15:3-4. What is the gospel?

Q. What does quicken mean?

Q. How does this verse line up with the gospel?

NOTES

Ye are of God, little children, and have overcome them: because greater is he that is in you, than he that is in the world. (1 John 4:4)

Q. Who are the little children?

Q. Who are the them?

Q. Who dwells in us who is greater than he that is in the world?

I can do all things through Christ which strengtheneth me. (Philippians 4:13)

Christ in me and me in Him is the key. Through Christ and in Christ, in the power of the Holy Spirit, I can plan a life free from addiction, and I can succeed.

But seek ye first the kingdom of God, and his righteousness; and all these things shall be added unto you. (Matthew 6:33)

Q. In light of all the things you have learned in Step 5, what does this verse mean to you?

Founder's Notes with Illustrations for Step 5

Step 5 – <u>Acknowledge</u>: Before God, others, and myself, I acknowledge my inventory to be true. I now begin to use the information from my inventory, formulating a plan that will result in a life set free from addiction.

Founder's Note 1, Step 5:

In Step 5 we go from looking at game films to getting into the game. For the first time for many of us, we are going on the offense. Again, I stress the need for a true and fearless inventory. I enlisted in the navy during the Vietnam War and was trained as a radar man/electronic warfare specialist. One of my tasks during ocean maneuvers was to recommend a course and speed to the bridge, which would enable the ship to turn into the wind while escorting carriers launching aircraft. One time when I was called upon to make this recommendation, I hurried too much and did not recheck my result before sending it to our captain on the bridge. My calculations turned out to be wrong, and the captain chastised me by looking me in the eye and saying, "No dope is better than bum dope." The same is true with our inventory.

Founder's Note 2, Step 5:

It is important to note that while we are thinking about our inventory, we are using our imaginations in the way God intended us to use them. Sinful thoughts lead to a rehearsal, which leads to acting out, which results in consequences. Godly thoughts lead to a plan, which leads to the constructing and carrying out of that plan, which results in the attainment of the object of our plan. If we plan out a life free of addiction, with God's help we will create that life.

Founder's Note 3, Step 5:

While formulating our inventory, we must identify triggers, those things that launch us into the rehearsal stage, which will eventually lead us to using again. Some triggers can be avoided, but other triggers need to be overcome. For example, as an alcoholic, I may be able to avoid going past bars by taking a different route home. However, I cannot prevent the Budweiser blimp from flying into my view. Some triggers are avoidable, but some are not. Avoiding the avoidable should be part of our plan.

Founder's Note 4, Step 5:

In the movie *Patton*, which starred George C. Scott, Patton defeated his Nazi counterpart, Rommel, by first reading Rommel's book on tank warfare. By doing this, Patton understood the way his enemy thought, and he was able to counteract Rommel's maneuvers and defeat him. It is important that we understand our enemy's thought process as well.

The enemy I am talking about here is humanism. Humanism seeks to elevate man to the same status as God. It is a form of religion that teaches the ultimate perfection of man. This is not a new thought. The Greek philosophers agreed with and sought after the perfection of man. However, the roots of humanism as we know it today can be traced to the Age of Enlightenment, which was a cultural movement of intellectuals in the eighteenth century. The Age of Enlightenment, also known as the Age of Reason, started in Europe and quickly spread to the Americas. Its purpose was to redefine society by the advancement of reason and science.

Jean-Jacques Rousseau was one of the intellectuals who helped advance this movement. In his treatise "On the Social Contract," Rousseau wrote that "Man is born free, and everywhere he is in chains." This quote is meant to tickle our ears by appealing to our humanity. When I took a course at Akron University on the history of western civilization, I was required to memorize that line. Yet the reasoning behind Rousseau's statement was sinister in nature and led to the bloody event in history known as the French Revolution. What Rousseau and others like him were saying is that man is born morally good but is then corrupted and restricted by the practices of society (such as religion, tradition, and government). This thought flies in the face of the biblical doctrine of original sin.

The theory of evolution takes the place of the biblical account of creation. As a result, we are taught that mankind has evolved from apes, rather than being taught the biblical view that we are all created in the image of God. God, in the view of those who believed as Rousseau, is replaced by reason and science. Therefore, man must overthrow the norms of society and embrace the idea of a utopian state. Humanism is being taught in the public schools today and is the driving force behind the intellectualism of many well-known college professors and teachers.

When I was in the fourth grade, my teacher asked my class if we thought we were born good or bad. I thought this to be a very foolish question indeed; naturally, I was born good. I would think this would be the answer of any young child who would be asked this question. However, now I see the question in its intended light. My teacher knew exactly what she was trying to accomplish in our young minds. She was encouraging us to think in a way that was directly opposite to the biblical point of view. The Bible states time and again that we are born sinners. This teacher was planting the seeds of humanism into the fertile soil of the young minds before her.

Founder's Note 5, Step 5:

We must also beware how the humanists will argue to advance their agenda. Their method is to take a little truth wrapped in a big lie and try to get you to accept the whole thought. If you do not accept what they say, they attack you with the little truth and accuse you of being heartless, prejudiced, homophobic, racist, and a host of other things.

For example, I heard a famous conservative radio talk show host debating with a humanist about whether or not prayer should be allowed back in schools. The humanist's argument for removing prayer from school was that kids make fun of kids who do not want to pray, and it is not right for those kids to be ridiculed. "Everyone," this humanist said, "has been made fun of, and it's a terrible thing to have happen to you when you're a child." When the talk show host disagreed, the humanist attacked him by saying, "Oh, so you think it's all right for kids to make fun of other kids?" This is twisted logic and it is twisted intentionally. The truth is that kids who are doing the teasing should be reprimanded for their teasing. They should be taught to respect the views of others. Prayer does not need to be removed. Adults who tolerate bullying may need to be removed.

When I played football, the coaches would call me names, embarrass me, and put a foot up my behind if they thought it would make me a better player. I did not like it at the time, but I learned a valuable lesson about perseverance and how to overcome adversity. I never once suggested they take football out of school.

Founder's Note 6, Step 5:

The unholy trinity is made up of the flesh, Satan, and the world. The unholy trinity is of one accord, and its goal is to destroy mankind. We are born in the image of God; therefore, we are the enemy of this unholy trinity.

While I was in school, I disliked a certain boy who picked on me. Later, I found myself disliking another young man I had never even met. I could not understand why until it dawned on me how much this young man resembled that boy in school. We are made in the image of God, and when that image begins to shine through, we will be hated by the enemies of God. The biggest feather in the devil's cap is when he deceives people who are made in God's image and precious in God's sight into taking their own lives.

Founder's Note 7, Step 5:

C. S. Lewis described Christianity as a fighting religion. The true story of the defeat of the German Sixth Army Division at Stalingrad, a turning point in World War II, illustrates our battle against the unholy trinity. Most of the battle for Stalingrad was fought in the city itself. It was the most brutal and feared type of combat, as the combatants fought house-to-house, door-to-door, and hand-to-hand. It was attack and counterattack, during which buildings would often change hands. The Germans would attack and expel the Soviets from a building only to be counterattacked and expelled themselves. The same buildings would be contested for, won, and lost several times during the course of a single day! The loss of life on both sides was staggering. In the end, the Soviets won the battle, which turned the tide of the entire war.

Spiritual warfare is like this, too. We begin our attack by beating back Satan, the world, and self (flesh). They counterattack. We advance, fall back, or make our stand. Back and forth we go. Inch by inch we take back the ground that Satan had claimed for his own. The battle makes us stronger. Our victory is assured.

Founder's Note 8, Step 5:

We should attempt to plant good seed every day. The good seed will gradually overcome the bad seed that we had planted in the past. It will overcome inch by inch, yard by yard, and acre by acre, until the bad seed has no more room to grow.

Founder's Note 9, Step 5:

When I got out of prison, I remember trying to apologize to my oldest daughter, Wendy, for failing to be a good father to her. She said, "That's all right Dad; life is all about choices, and you made some bad ones." God can take what we meant to do as evil and use it for His glory. He is using my testimony as proof positive that He can and will change lives. He will help us to make the right choices, and as a result, the right things happen.

A young lady in our church asked if I would stand with her in court and be her character witness. This young lady had abused drugs to the point that she was on probation, had been divorced, and had lost custody of her son. She then gave her life to Christ and began attending church.

Her probation officer decided that she had turned her life around enough to be allowed visitation rights. The first time she went to visit her son, she went alone, which turned out to be a mistake, because her ex-husband was resentful of her new life and circumstances. He falsely accused her of being argumentative and abusive toward him, and he called the police. She was arrested and taken to the police station, where she had to post bond in order to be released. A court date was set, and that was when she called me.

It seems to me that a person in their right mind would not ask a three-time-convicted felon to stand up with them in court as a character reference, but that is what she asked me to do. On the day of her hearing, before we entered the courtroom, she expressed her thoughts to me. She told me that simply due to her past, she believed she would have to accept a plea bargain. She feared going to jail on a parole violation and losing the visitation rights she had worked so hard to achieve.

Not long after we had entered the courtroom, the judge called her up. I stood at her side while the judge apologized to her. He said this charge was hearsay and should never have come before him. He said that the person who had made the charges did so out of jealousy and contempt. I remember the judge relating to the bailiff how this young lady had been forced to put up a large sum of money for bail, and he wanted the money returned to her before she left that day. Again he apologized, and then he dropped all the charges. Walking out of the courtroom, she turned to me in wonder and said, "Nothing ever went right for me before." What was the difference? She had given her life to the Lord. When you choose to serve God, all your choices become better, and good things begin to happen.

Founder's Note 10, Step 5:

To pursue the flesh is to covet the things and pleasures of this world. This perpetual state never stops. I once heard Joyce Meyers teach about lust and the desires of the flesh. She said that the flesh could never be satisfied. She used herself as an example. After she had been on a diet for several weeks and lost several pounds, someone brought a box of donuts into the office. The donuts enticed her and the flesh tempted her, saying, "Go ahead, Joyce; you know you want to eat one of those. Hey! You deserve it, you've been good. One donut isn't going to kill you." She gave in to the temptation and ate a donut. Her flesh then accused her by saying, "Why did you do that? You know you're overweight!" That is how the flesh works. It entices and then accuses and is never satisfied. I am convinced that hell is a place of perpetual want.

Founder's Note 11, Step 5:

The trick to overcoming the flesh is to see things through the eyes of the eternal. The desires of this world are temporal. For example, when I got out of prison for the third time, I was digging through some boxes that had been stored in the basement of my parents' home. The first thing I took out of one of the boxes was a briefcase. This briefcase was made of the finest leather and had cost eight hundred dollars at the time I wrote the bad check for it. You see, I just had to have it. However, after the briefcase had been in the basement for so long, it was no longer shiny black and supple. Instead, it was gray and cracked like a wallet that had been soaked and dried out in the sun.

The next thing I took out of the box was an eight-track tape player. This was December 2001. No one listened to eight-track tapes anymore, but at the time, I thought I had to have it, so I wrote another bad check. In case you did not know, purposely writing bad checks is the same as stealing. I stole those items. Why? Because my flesh told me that I deserved them and had to have them. The only thing I really deserved, though, was the prison sentence that the judge gave me.

I get a kick out of the car commercials on television that tell people to come on down and get the credit they deserve. That is exactly what they are going to get: the credit they deserve. The truth is, I did not need the things for which I had written the bad checks. Looking through the eyes of the eternal, I can see that they had no real lasting value. What I needed instead was a relationship with God. That is the only thing that really matters and has eternal worth. God does not offer us what we deserve. Instead, He offers us new life in Christ.

Founder's Note 12, Step 5:

Corrie ten Boom, Ravensbrück death-camp survivor and author of *The Hiding Place,* said we are to hold all things loosely, because all things belong to God. He can ask for them back at any time. This even includes our children.

Step 6

Change

> **I** am willing to change
> and to allow God to change me.

(Discuss each Bible verse by asking, "How does this particular verse apply to Step 6?")

Note: If you have seen yourself for who you really are, then you have seen the need to change. The problem is, it is very difficult for us to allow change to happen without our control or direction. But that is exactly what needs to take place. We need to allow the Holy Spirit, who now lives within us, to empower and direct the change that is taking place within us. This cannot be done without surrendering our wills. Surrendering our wills is not just a one-time thing. It needs to be done on a daily, and at times, even on an hourly basis.

Q. Why is it difficult to see ourselves for who we truly are?

Q. Why is it not possible for us to do the changing that needs to take place?

Q. How does taking a daily inventory (Step 5) tie in with the concept of becoming willing to change and to allow God to do the changing?

Q. Why could surrendering be an hourly process?

Q. What does surrendering have to do with making the right choices?

> *For it is God which worketh in you both to will and to do of his good pleasure.*
> (Philippians 2:13)

Q. Whose work within us results in our being changed?

Q. Why is it hard for us to accept that change?

Q. What does surrender have to do with change?

NOTES

Q. What does both to will and to do mean to you?

A. God changes our will to be in accord with what He wills for us. We then begin to do those things God wills us to do.

Q. What do you think God's good pleasure is concerning you?

Note: As Christians, we believe in the triune God, or the Holy Trinity. The Holy Trinity consists of three persons: Father, Son, and Holy Ghost (Spirit). These three are of one accord. They cannot contradict each other. We receive our new nature when we are born again, and that new nature is in one accord with the triune God. The struggle then begins between our new nature and our old nature. The struggle itself is a sign that we are saved.

> Repent ye therefore, and be converted, that your sins may be blotted out, when the times of refreshing shall come from the presence of the Lord. (Acts 3:19)

Q. What does repent mean?

Q. What does be converted mean?

A. To be changed into a different form.[8]

Q. What is the difference between being converted and being saved?

A. Salvation begins the conversion process.

Q. What are the times of refreshing?

Q. Where do the times of refreshing originate?

> Then will I sprinkle clean water upon you, and ye shall be clean: from all your filthiness, and from all your idols, will I cleanse you. A new heart also will I give you, and a new spirit will I put within you: and I will take away the stony heart out of your flesh, and I will give you an heart of flesh. And I will put my spirit within you, and cause you to walk in my statutes, and ye shall keep my judgments, and do them. And ye shall dwell in the land that I gave to your fathers; and ye shall be my people, and I will be your God. (Ezekiel 36:25-28)

Note: This is the conversion process. What a tremendous promise we have from God! This should excite us and make us want to change all the more. God's

---

8   http://www.dictionary.com/browse/converted?s=t.

work is perfect; we need to let Him work. How long the process of change takes within us is directly proportional to the extent of our surrender.

Q. What are idols?

A. Something or someone that takes priority or precedence over God.

Q. Can you name some idols an addict may have?

Note: As addicts, we became indifferent to the needs of others. We also became insensitive to the pain and loss that we had inflicted on others. God promises to change our hearts. We can again feel what it is to love people. Would you like to care about others again?

> *Verily I say unto you, Except ye be converted, and become as little children, ye shall not enter into the kingdom of heaven.* (Matthew 18:3)

Q. Why the use of the adjective little here and not just become as children?

A. The smaller the child, the more he depends upon his parents.

Note: This is another verse that is often misunderstood. This verse is not about innocence. A child is born with a sinful nature. For example; a child does not need to be taught to lie but does need to be taught to tell the truth. You can see the sinful nature of children when you put several children in a room with only one toy. Have you noticed that one of the first words a child learns to say is "mine"?

Rather than being about innocence, this verse is about dependence. Little children rely on their parents for all their needs. They trust their parents to provide for them. In the same way, God wants us to rely solely on Him. He wants us to trust in His provision. The greater the extent of our dependence upon God, the greater the extent of our surrender to God.

> *Turn you at my reproof: behold, I will pour out my spirit unto you, I will make known my words unto you.* (Proverbs 1:23)

Q. How would you define reproof?

Q. Is reproof a good thing or a bad thing? (Discuss)

Q. How does God make His words known to us?

> *Let the wicked forsake his way, and the unrighteous man his thoughts: and let him return unto the LORD, and he will have mercy upon him; and to our God, for he will abundantly pardon.* (Isaiah 55:7)

NOTES

Note: The partnership has two parts. On our part we choose to turn from unrighteousness and return to the Lord; on God's part (out of His mercy) He will forgive us (not because we deserve forgiveness, but because it is God's nature to forgive), and we will be abundantly pardoned. This is a promise from God. It is certain that God will do His part. If we lack God's pardon, it is because we have chosen not to do our part. Life is all about choices.

> *Search me, O God, and know my heart: try me, and know my thoughts: and see if there be any wicked way in me, and lead me in the way everlasting.* (Psalm 139:23-24)

Q. Who is the psalmist asking to search him? This is a very brave request.

Q. Can sin hide itself from the sinner?

Q. Whose way would be the way everlasting?

Note: *Try me* does not mean *tempt me*, but instead it means check me out, see if I have any flaws, and see if there is anything within me that God does not want there. God's ways are perfect and they are infinite in their perfection. They will never be replaced, nor can they ever be improved upon.

> *Shew me thy ways, O Lord; teach me thy paths. Lead me in thy truth, and teach me: for thou art the God of my salvation; on thee do I wait all the day. Remember, O Lord, thy tender mercies and thy loving-kindnesses; for they have been ever of old. Remember not the sins of my youth, nor my transgressions: according to thy mercy remember thou me for thy goodness' sake, O Lord. Good and upright is the Lord: therefore will he teach sinners in the way.* (Psalm 25:4-8)

Q. Who does the Bible say leads us into truth?

Q. Whose goodness is the psalmist appealing to here?

Q. Who does the teaching?

> *The law of the Lord is perfect, converting the soul: the testimony of the Lord is sure, making wise the simple.* (Psalm 19:7)

Note: When we set the Word of God as our standard and we hold all things up to its light before we make any decisions, then our judgments will be correct. We do not need a college degree to make good decisions or to do the right thing. There is tremendous wisdom in the Bible, and when we tap into that wisdom, we are made wise indeed.

*If he turn not, he will whet his sword; he hath bent his bow, and
made it ready.* (Psalm 7:12)

Note: This is a warning to those who choose not to turn from their sin and who
continue along the path of the unrighteous. God is the one whetting His sword
and bending His bow to let the arrows fly. The unrighteous are His target. God
does not miss.

*Have I any pleasure at all that the wicked should die? saith the
Lord God: and not that he should return from his ways, and live?*
(Ezekiel 18:23)

Q. Does the Lord take pleasure in punishing us?

Q. Who is doing the choosing here?

Q. What are the two choices presented in the above passage?

Q. Which one did you choose?

*Stand fast therefore in the liberty wherewith Christ hath made
us free, and be not entangled again with the yoke of bondage.*
(Galatians 5:1)

Q. What does it mean to stand fast?

Q. Name some ways a Christian can get entangled in bondage again even though
Christ died to set him free.

A. Sin and legalism. (Discuss)

*Being confident of this very thing, that he which hath begun a
good work in you will perform it until the day of Jesus Christ.*
(Philippians 1:6)

Q. Who is doing the change within you?

Q. Will He complete the change?

Q. How long will He perform the change?

Q. What would be another word we could use for confident here?

NOTES

For a little change of pace:

Note: The verse below is to be used as a Bible study which will take up two entire meetings. Have fun with it; you will be excited about what you are able to get out of it.

Many times we read a verse and think we have its meaning; we move on without really meditating on the verse, but in reality we do not understand the verse at all. We just think we do. Let's use Ephesians 5:21 as an example and see what we can glean from a careful and thoughtful study of God's Word. This is a command from God, and as such, I need to have a complete understanding of what God is telling me to do here. My new nature is to please God. I want to do what God asks me to do. Therefore, I need to understand fully what He is asking me to do in this verse.

The goal of this study is to break down the Greek words for *submitting* and *fear* to their lowest common denominators. When you do this with the word *submitting,* you will find all the attributes of what a Christian should be. You will also find out that there is more to fearing God than just reverential awe. You will need a dry-erase board, a concordance, and a good dictionary. Group participation and discussion should be encouraged.

> *Submitting yourselves one to another in the fear of God.*
> (Ephesians 5:21)

Q. Which two words in this verse might we not know their meanings?

Q. Define submitting by breaking it down derivative by derivative to its simplest understandable form. (Use the form on the next page.)

Q. Define fear by finding its simplest understandable derivative. (Use the form on the next page.)

Q. What have you learned from your study of Ephesians 5:21?

Submitting	Fear	NOTES

Need some help? See the "Breaking It Down" addendum.

NOTES

Founder's Notes with Illustrations for Step 6

Step 6 – <u>Change</u>: I am willing to change and to allow God to change me.

Founder's Note 1, Step 6:

God does not want to change someone who is unwilling to be changed; however, the extent to which we are willing to change is directly proportional to our Christian growth. I use two examples here. The first example is of the potter and the clay. The potter forms his clay on a potter's wheel. He uses the centrifugal force of the spinning clay to produce the friction needed for the potter to shape the clay by applying pressure with his hands and fingers, achieving the end product. A good potter is dexterous.

What would happen if the clay had a mind of its own? What if the clay refused to submit to the pressure being applied by the potter? What if the clay decided to do its own thing and go its own way? The result would be a mess. Eventually, the potter would have to throw the clay back into a shapeless lump; the clay would be useless. I think this allegorically sums up the life of an addict – a life lived in open disobedience and rebellion to God.

The second example is that of author Phillip Yancey, who stated that after his conversion to Christianity, he expected God to do big things through him. He expected God to transform him into a great saint like Francis of Assisi. Thirty years later, though, he is still Phillip Yancey, the only difference being his growing dependence on God. Mr. Yancey equated his growth as a Christian with learning to rely on God. To him, and to me, they are directly proportional.

Founder's Note 2, Step 6:

The problem we have as we begin to read and mature in our understanding of God's Word is applying what we have learned to others instead of to ourselves. We want to change those around us, but we remain unwilling to change ourselves. I learned early in my Christian walk that it was a lot easier for me to see the faults of others than to find fault with myself. When I began attending church services in prison, I would notice guys sitting in front of me holding hands and treating church like they were out on a date. I would also notice inmates who were acting very holy in church, but I knew that they were anything but holy back in the dorms.

This started to bother me, and before I knew it, I was seeing hypocrisy everywhere. I was beginning to feel that church was not the place for me. Then I had the idea to move to the front row, putting behind me all the things that were distracting me. I determined to focus on Christ, knowing He would never let me down. I began to realize that church was a place for sinners to go and I was as much a sinner as anyone else. Church is not a perfect place; it becomes less perfect when I walk through the door. Do not let what others do keep you from going to church. We all need to hear the Word of God. Hearing and reading the Word of God changes us. During the six years that I was saved and in prison, I read my Bible for thousands of hours, and that is not an understatement. God's

Word cleanses us and begins the transformational process needed to conform us into the image of God's Son.

Founder's Note 3, Step 6:

It is always good to interject a little humor while teaching. I find that the best humor is the jest pointed at oneself. For instance, while discussing why it is hard for us to see ourselves for who we truly are, I mention that for forty years I looked in the mirror and saw Brad Pitt. When I saw myself for who I truly was, it hurt. The truth hurts, and that is why we turn away from reality and instead turn to a make-believe world of our own invention. I asked God, "Why this face? Why me?" Now, though, I am happy with the face God has given me; it works for me. God's way is always best.

Founder's Note 4, Step 6:

We need to be careful regarding the subject of change. God changes everyone according to His plan and purpose for that individual. We who are saved tend to forget how long it took us to change, and we tend to expect others to change overnight. Also, we tend to want to conform newborn Christians into our own image rather than allowing the Holy Spirit to conform the person into the image of God's Son. Then there are those who set unrealistically high expectations for themselves, and when they do not measure up to those expectations, the devil instills in them a sense of guilt and failure that results in their loss of joy.

Martin Luther and John Wesley both wrote about setting such high expectations and failing to the point that they actually began to hate God. They were finally set free when they came to the realization that it was all about grace and not about pleasing God in the flesh. It is not about what we do for God, but what God did for us. I believe that if the Holy Spirit of God dwells in you, He is going to produce a change in you. You can resist the change and go kicking and screaming, or you can accept the change without resisting; but change you will. An apple tree glorifies God when it produces apples, as it was created to do. It does not stand in the farmer's field grunting and groaning, saying, "I am going to produce one hundred apples today." No, the apple tree produces fruit because it is its nature to produce fruit. A Christian will produce fruit, as well. This is the fruit of the Spirit. It is going to be a natural result of who we are. Change will happen, and in many instances, others will see the change before we do.

Founder's Note 5, Step 6:

In Acts 4:13 we read, *Now when they saw the boldness of Peter and John, and perceived that they were unlearned and ignorant men, they marveled; and they took knowledge of them, that they had been with Jesus.* These Sadducees, priests, and scribes had received a lifetime of education, had attended all the right universities, and had studied under all the right professors. They knew all the right people and attended all the affluent dinner parties, yet they looked at two simple fishermen from Galilee and marveled at them. Why? They had been with Jesus. Peter and John had been changed, and the change was obvious, even to

NOTES

those outside the faith. They were changed men because they had been with Jesus Christ, who had taught them, discipled them, and set the personal standard from which they were to model their lives. If you have been with Jesus, then you have been changed too. If you have not been changed, then you have not been with Jesus.

Founder's Note 6, Step 6:

Acts 4:14 says, *"And beholding the man which was healed* [the formerly crippled beggar] *standing with them* [Peter and John], *they* [the religious rulers] *could say nothing against it.* The rulers of the synagogue were upset; they thought they had heard the name of Jesus for the last time, yet here it was again. They wanted to deny that Jesus could heal, that He could save, that He could change a person forever and make that person whole – not just physically but spiritually, too.

As addicts, we have lied so convincingly and so often that no one who knows us is going to believe us when we say that we are born again and have been changed. Non-believers will not understand the transforming power of the Holy Spirit. Believers will hold back their judgment and watch and wait. Can you blame them? I have been asked several times to counsel people who have loved ones getting out of prison or a rehab center. They want to know what to do, how to act, and what to believe. After all, addicts are very good at laying down a guilt trip when those they love express doubt about what the addicts are doing. My advice to the family is to believe what you see and not what you hear.

The religious rulers could not deny the change in the once-crippled man who stood before them healed. That is what addicts must do to reestablish trust. They must stand before the world whole. They must live out before doubting eyes a life centered on Christ. How many times have I heard the term *jailhouse Christian*? There are no jailhouse Christians; there are only believers and unbelievers, those who have been changed and those who have not been changed.

After I had been released from prison, I remember praying, "Lord, if You give my family back to me, I will praise You; but if You don't give my family back to me, I will still praise You. This is what my life is all about – praising You." Live out the change God has wrought in you. Stay focused on Jesus, and sooner or later even your harshest skeptic will have to acknowledge that you have changed for the better; when they do, make sure to share with them the One who did the changing.

Founder's Note 7, Step 6:

Psalm 37 tells us that God gives us the desires of our hearts. This does not mean that He is a genie and all you need to do is rub a lamp to be granted three wishes. I guarantee we would wish for the wrong things. God changes what *we* want into what *He* wants. As a result, we pray for what He wants us to pray for, because He develops within us a very strong desire for those things. Then, He grants us those things for which we prayed. This causes the desired effect, that we develop an attitude of gratitude toward God. We desire the things He wants us to have; we pray for those things; God answers our prayers, and we thank Him for it.

Founder's Note 8, Step 6:

Concerning the times of refreshing, I use an example taken from my navy days. I was going through boot camp at the Great Lakes base in Chicago. During our training, one of the things we learned was that it is possible for a steel ship to catch on fire, and that once steel begins to burn, it is very hard to put out. To simulate a fire in the lower sections of a ship, fuel oil was set on fire in cement block bunkers. We were then designated into teams, assigned hoses, and sent into the block building to put out the fire. I remember how black everything was and how the smoke filled and burned my lungs. Then we pulled back the levers, and the smoke was thrown back by the heavy stream of water coming out of the hoses. The air was fresher and my lungs no longer burned. The spray from the water actually blew back into my face, and I felt refreshed.

That is how it is to be lost and going through the world. It seems that the air is toxic. It seems hard to breathe. The world is out to suffocate us. All around us, things are withering and dying, but the indwelling of the Holy Spirit changes all that. The world is no longer a threat to me. If God be for me, who can be against me? I am no longer choking on my own vomit. I have been rescued and placed on the mountaintop where the air is fresh and clean. These are the times of refreshing, the times of being born again to do the will of God.

Founder's Note 9, Step 6:

In his book *At the Altar of Sexual Idolatry*, Steve Gallagher writes: "Deeply embedded within the heart of man is a spiritual altar. Every human being has the capacity – no, the need – to worship. The objects of that worship are the things or persons which have taken the preeminent position of importance in the person's life. Whatever they may be, they cast their looming shadow over all of the other aspects of his life." Gallagher goes on to write that this is the position in a person's heart that God demands to occupy. However, as fallen men we tend to worship and bow down to anything but the rightful occupant – God.

In Genesis, we are told that man was created as the steward of the earth. God is our boss and we are to bow down to nothing that has been created; we are to bow only to God. To bow down to something is to relinquish control of one's life to whatever we are bowing to. We are no longer in the driver's seat. An idol drives us, determines where we go, what we do, who we hang out with, and what we think. If God is in the driver's seat, you will find us in church or at a church event hanging out with God's people or simply sitting at home reading God's Word. If drugs are driving us, you will find us in a drug-infested neighborhood, hanging out with other drug addicts, competing for whatever product is out there for us to use.

Founder's Note 10, Step 6:

I believe it has been proven that knowledge can be transmitted genetically. I am not talking about scientific theories or algebraic formulas or the like, but I am told that a child born today is actually smarter than a child born hundreds of years ago. I do not know if this is true, but I believe it makes sense. Within all of us are two polar-opposite thoughts. The first is that we all have this sense of our own invincibility. There is a part of us that thinks we are indestructible. I think it would be hard to find young men to fight wars if they knew for certain that they were going to be killed. There is something within us that thinks things always happen to the other guy and not to us. Could this be a genetic remnant of thought retained from the days when we walked with God in the garden, before sin and death entered into the world?

The second thought is that we have some innate drive to destroy ourselves. Drug addicts will tell you they know that what they are doing will kill them, but they just don't care. An alcoholic will tell you that alcohol is killing him, yet he will drink all the harder as a result. We know that cigarette smoking is deadly, yet many people smoke several packs a day. What possesses people to commit suicide vicariously through their addictions? Could this be a genetic remnant of the original sin of Adam? Sin seeks to destroy us. God seeks to give us life and to give it eternally.

Founder's Note 11, Step 6:

Proud people do not want to hear any kind of reproof. Either they think they are always right, or they know they are wrong but do not want to change. I once heard someone say, "Never offer anyone advice. A wise man doesn't need it and a fool won't receive it." I would describe that as two ends of a spectrum, and certainly there are a lot of people in the middle who heed sound advice. The thing that prevents many people from heeding good advice is pride. Many times in the Bible, God refers to His people as being stiff-necked. This is actually a picture of someone trying to turn a horse by using a halter and reins. We had ponies when I was young, and I know that horses have very strong, long, large neck muscles. You can't turn a horse if he does not want to be turned. God's people are like that.

Founder's Note 12, Step 6:

Sin can hide itself from the sinner. With our pride and self-centeredness, we see the sin in others and pass judgment on them, while totally ignoring sin within ourselves. I think the Lord knew this when He commanded us to love our neighbors as ourselves. We can forgive ourselves of almost anything, but let our neighbors transgress against us just a little and it is "Katy, bar the door!" Sin is deceitful and can make us feel like we are in control, when in fact it is orchestrating our every move. There is no such thing as a little sin, just as there is no such thing as a little cancer cell.

Step 7

Ask

> I humbly ask God to forgive me and to change me through the power of His Holy Spirit.

(Discuss each Bible verse by asking, "How does this particular verse apply to Step 7?")

Note: God wants to forgive us and transform us into the image of His Son. How slowly or quickly that transformation takes place depends a lot on how humble we remain. We need to walk in God's forgiveness, knowing that some people will never forgive us for what we have done. However, if the God of all creation forgives us, we can and will step out into eternity with that forgiveness.

According to Step 7:

Q. What does it mean to be humble?

Q. Who does the changing?

Q. Who should get the credit for the change?

Q. How does giving God the credit help to keep us humble?

Q. How does giving God the credit help us to acquire the attitude of gratitude towards God?

Q. Who does the forgiving?

Q. Do we deserve to be forgiven?

> *If we say that we have no sin, we deceive ourselves, and the truth is not in us. If we confess our sins, he is faithful and just to forgive us our sins, and to cleanse us from all unrighteousness. If we say that we have not sinned, we make him a liar, **and his word is not in us**. (1 John 1:8-10)*

Q. Is it possible to deceive ourselves? If so, give some examples.

NOTES

Q. What does it mean to confess?

A. To bring our minds to a state of agreement with the mind of God.

Q. Who is faithful and who is just?

Q. Who does the cleansing?

Q. Is saying that we have not sinned a sign of spiritual/religious pride?

Q. Do you view yourself as a sinner or as a non-sinner?

Note: The hardest person to change is the one who does not see a need to change. According to worldly standards, there are many good people in the world. Many of these people think they are good enough to get to heaven. God has told us in Isaiah 55 that His ways are not our ways. What does the Bible say about people being good enough to get to heaven on their own merits? To confess means to bring your mind into accord with the mind of God. God is not going to change; you need to change by the renewing of your mind.

> For I acknowledge my transgressions: and my sin is ever before me.
> (Psalm 51:3)

Q. Who wrote this psalm?

Q. What are transgressions?

Q. To what terrible transgressions is David confessing?

Q. Against whom had David transgressed?

Q. What do you think David meant when he wrote, My sin is ever before me?

Note: It is a good thing to remember the condition we were in when God saved us. It is good to keep our sins ever before us so we do not become religiously proud. However, we also need to remember that God has forgiven us, and our sins have been cleansed by the blood of Christ. When we remember how great our sins were, then we begin to understand the magnitude of the grace and mercy extended to us by God, which resulted in our being forgiven. This understanding should humble us and develop within us an attitude of gratitude.

> Now no chastening [during the transformation process] for the present seemeth to be joyous, but grievous: nevertheless afterward it yieldeth the peaceable fruit of righteousness unto them which are exercised thereby. (Hebrews 12:11)

Q. David was severely punished for his transgressions, yet he was grateful to God even when punished. Why? (Discuss)

> *But he giveth more grace. Wherefore he saith, God resisteth the proud, but giveth grace unto the humble.* (James 4:6)

Review: What does the acronym GRACE stand for?

Q. To whom is God in direct opposition?

Q. Who is a receiver of God's grace?

Q. Can you see how your past pride kept you from acknowledging your need for God?

Review:

Q. What are the two roots of any addiction?

Q. When we do our personal inventories, for what should we be looking?

Q. How often do we need to do these inventories?

Q. How do these inventories help develop a spirit of humility within us?

> *Pride goeth before destruction, and an haughty spirit before a fall. Better it is to be of an humble spirit with the lowly, than to divide the spoil with the proud.* (Proverbs 16:18-19)

Q. Do you see how pride led you to where you are today? (Discuss)

Q. What does haughty mean?

A. Disdainfully proud, arrogant.[9]

Q. How would you define spoil?

A. Booty, loot, or plunder.[10]

Q. There is an alternative being offered here, which means we need to make a choice. What is the alternative being offered? What choice do we need to make? (Discuss)

---

9   http://www.dictionary.com/browse/haughty?s=t.
10   http://www.dictionary.com/browse/spoil?s=t.

NOTES

Note: The term *destruction* here refers not only to our own destruction but also to the destruction of those who have been damaged as a result of our prideful conditions (many of our families have been destroyed). Addiction creates an atmosphere of destruction. Can you relate what has happened in your life to the above verse and make application?

> *For by grace are ye saved through faith; and that not of your-selves: it is the gift of God: not of works, lest any man should boast.* (Ephesians 2:8-9)

Q. What is the meaning of works?

A. Doing things in an attempt to earn our way into heaven.

Q. What is the difference between how works is used here and its usage in James 2:17-18? Look up the verses and discuss.

Note: Ephesians 2:8-9 are two of the most important verses in the Bible. We need to understand the meaning of these verses thoroughly, completely, and without conditions if we are to remove pride, one of the primary roots of our addiction. God created us with the cognitive ability to believe. He also provided us with the person in whom we need to place our belief. He supplies us with the grace necessary for our salvation. None of this has anything to do with our abilities, nor does it have anything to do with something we have earned. We cannot make God a debtor to us; rather, we are in debt to Him.

Q. Can you think of ways we would try to take credit for our own salvation?

Q. Do any of those ways have merit when presented before a holy God?

> *Now faith is the substance of things hoped for, the evidence of things not seen.* (Hebrews 11:1)

Q. What is faith?

A. A belief or conviction that a thing is true.

Q. What is the meaning of substance?

A. Foundation, substructure, that from which something is made. Assurance.

> *And this is the record, that God hath given to us eternal life, and this life is in his Son.* (1 John 5:11)

Q. What do you think is meant by the record?

A. A historical fact based in truth that cannot be disproven.

> *Neither is there salvation in any other: for there is none other name under heaven given among men, whereby we must be saved.* (Acts 4:12)

Note: The above verse is from God's Word, and God's Word is true. We have led lives that have not acknowledged God in the slightest. We have openly sinned against Him. We have embraced sin as a way of life, stubbornly refusing to acknowledge God as Lord of our lives. Yet isn't it just like us to complain that there is only one name upon which we can call for salvation? Isn't it just like us to look for a way other than the one God has provided? The truth be told, we do not deserve to be saved at all. (Discuss)

> *Who hath saved us, and called us with an holy calling, not according to our works, but according to his own purpose and grace, which was given us in Christ Jesus before the world began, but is now made manifest by the appearing of our Saviour Jesus Christ, who hath abolished death, and hath brought life and immortality to light through the gospel.* (2 Timothy 1:9-10)

Q. Who has saved us?

Q. Who has called us?

Q. For what are we called?

Q. What do you think this holy calling is?

Q. To whose purpose are we called?

Q. Did we earn this calling?

Q. What does before the world began mean to you?

Q. How would you paraphrase the term made manifest?

Review:

Define the gospel.

   What is the gift of the gospel?

> *If my people, which are called by my name, shall humble themselves, and pray, and seek my face, and turn from their wicked ways; then will I hear from heaven, and will forgive their sin, and will heal their land.* (2 Chronicles 7:14)

NOTES

Q. To whom is God speaking here?

Q. If God's people were already humble, would there be a need to tell them to humble themselves?

Q. In light of what is written here, do you think God hears a proud person?

Q. How could pride inhibit us from praying?

Q. How does this verse apply to Step 7?

> He hath shewed thee, O man, what is good; and what doth the Lord require of thee, but to do justly, and to love mercy, and to walk humbly with thy God? (Micah 6:8)

Q. In the above verse, what does require mean?

A. To place under an obligation.[11]

Q. What are the three things that God requires of us?

Q. Is it possible to fulfill these requirements without knowing Christ as Savior?

Q. Do we need to apply this verse to our daily lives if we are to be free from our addiction(s)?

> For thus saith the high and lofty One that inhabiteth eternity, whose name is Holy; I dwell in the high and holy place, with him also that is of a contrite and humble spirit, to revive the spirit of the humble, and to revive the heart of the contrite ones. (Isaiah 57:15)

Note: In this wonderful verse from Isaiah, God is describing Himself as only He can. We also get a little glimpse of heaven and those who inhabit it.

Q. Who is in the dwelling place of the Lord?

Q. What does contrite mean?

A. Showing sincere regret for wrongdoing.

Q. What do you think it means to be revived? (Discuss)

Q. Are there any proud people in heaven?

---

11   http://www.dictionary.com/browse/require?s=t.

Q. If we want to dwell with God in His high and holy place for all eternity, in what condition do our hearts and spirits need to be?

Founder's Notes with Illustrations for Step 7

Step 7 – <u>Ask</u>: I humbly ask God to forgive me and to change me through the power of His Holy Spirit.

Founder's Note 1, Step 7:

James 4:6 states, *But he giveth more grace. Wherefore he saith, God resisteth the proud, but giveth grace unto the humble.* According to this verse, if I want to be heard by God and if I truly want God to change me, then I should have a humble attitude in all things.

Founder's Note 2, Step 7:

How we approach God matters. Today's Christians often take the *abba/daddy* relationship way too far. We have an overfamiliarity with God that is very presumptuous in nature and is another manifestation of pride. As we have learned from our study of the word *fear* in Step 5, we are to approach God with respect and reverential awe. This is part of what it means to fear God. I remember calling my dad "daddy," but there were also times I called him "sir." I loved my dad, but I feared him too.

Founder's Note 3, Step 7:

In the Bible, the prophets were God's ambassadors. When they were acting in the capacity of their office they were speaking for God. When they spoke, it was as if God was speaking, and how they were treated was how God was treated. If the people persecuted a prophet, they were in actuality persecuting God. Below are two biblical examples I use to point out the improper way to approach God:

Then the king sent unto him a captain of fifty with his fifty. And he went up to him: and, behold, he sat on the top of an hill. And he spake unto him, Thou man of God, the king hath said, Come down. And Elijah answered and said to the captain of fifty, If I be a man of God, then let fire come down from heaven, and consume thee and thy fifty. And there came down fire from heaven, and consumed him and his fifty. Again also he sent unto him another captain of fifty with his fifty. And he answered and said unto him, O man of God, thus hath the king said, Come down quickly. And Elijah answered and said unto them, If I be a man of God, let fire come down from heaven, and consume thee and thy fifty. And the fire of God came down from heaven, and consumed him and his fifty. And he sent again a captain of the third fifty with his fifty. And the third captain of fifty went up, and came and fell on his knees before Elijah, and besought him, and said unto him, O man of God, I pray thee, let my life, and the life of these fifty thy servants, be precious in thy sight. Behold, there came fire down from heaven, and burnt up the two captains of the former fifties with their fifties: therefore let my life now be precious in thy sight. And the angel of the Lord said unto Elijah, Go down with him: be not afraid of him. And he arose, and went down with him unto the king. (2 Kings 1:9-15)

Notice how the third captain approached Elijah. Here is the second biblical example:

And he [Elisha] *went up from thence unto Bethel: and as he was going up by the way, there came forth little children out of the city, and mocked him, and said unto him, Go up, thou bald head; go up, thou bald head. And he turned back, and looked on them, and cursed them in the name of the Lord. And there came forth two she bears out of the wood, and tare forty and two children of them.* (2 Kings 2:23-24)

Galatians 6:7 tells us, *Be not deceived; God is not mocked: for whatsoever a man soweth, that shall he also reap.* We need to keep it real with God and approach Him with humility.

Founder's Note 4, Step 7:

In his *Chronicles of Narnia*, C. S. Lewis writes about some children on their way to meet a lion named Aslan. Upon learning that Aslan was a lion, the children asked if he was safe. The reply was, "Course he isn't safe. But he's good." This is also true of the lion of Judah. He is not safe, but He is good. We need to approach Him with that in mind.

Founder's Note 5, Step 7:

In numerous places in the Bible, God tells us to humble ourselves. I believe it is less painful for us to humble ourselves than to have God humble us. On one occasion while visiting Alabama, I made a friend who had a friend who managed a radio station. I was asked by my new friend, Jack, if I would allow the radio station to tape my testimony for public broadcast. The taping session went well; it went so well, in fact, that the station manager asked if I was speaking anywhere that evening. After I told him that I was sharing my testimony at a youth rally at Jack's church (Jack was the youth pastor of that church), the manager asked if he and his wife could attend. That is when the delusions of grandeur kicked in for me. I could envision myself as the next Charles Stanley, Tony Evans, or Chuck Swindoll. When time came for the evening rally, I found myself looking out the window and watching for that big-time radio producer and his wife to show up.

Right before the rally began, they came in and sat down. I paid little attention to the praise and worship groups that sang that evening. All I could think of was that this was my big chance. I would soon be famous, and my ministry would grow by leaps and bounds. No more waiting for checks to come in the mail; instead the checks would flow in by the hundreds, or so I thought.

Jack introduced me to the people at the rally. When I began speaking, I was looking right at the radio executive and his wife. I was thinking to myself, "Wait until you hear this!" What they heard that night was a man who could not remember even the simplest Bible verse. They heard a man who stuttered and stammered, who spoke incoherently, and who was out of sequence in his delivery, without any assistance from the Holy Spirit. I could not have embarrassed myself more if I had stood there naked.

The radio executive and his wife got up and left. I heard that still small voice saying to me, "If I wanted you to be on the radio, I would have put you on the radio. I brought you here to minister to these children." I was so ashamed that the tears began to flow, and as they flowed, my message strengthened, and I began to share with those kids what God had done and was still doing in my life. The message was no longer about me, but about the God who saved me. I went back to the heart of worship, and God blessed the rest of that night. Later that evening when I returned to my room, I cried out for God's forgiveness. I was ashamed before my God because I had cared more about myself than those children. I asked for His forgiveness, and He forgave me. God humbled me that night, and it was one of the most painful experiences I have gone through in the ministry. That is why I say it is better to humble yourself than to have God humble you.

Founder's Note 6, Step 7:

By the time we get to Step 7, we are beginning to acquire some knowledge of the Bible. We are beginning to understand who God is and what He expects from His people. We need to be careful, though. There is a lot of truth in the old adage, "A little knowledge is a dangerous thing." Knowledge can puff us up and make us proud. If we are not careful, we will exchange one form of arrogance for another. The people who received the strictest reprimand from Christ while He was on the earth were the Sadducees and Pharisees – the religious rulers of the day. Why? Because of their spiritual pride, they did not see their need to repent and change. They were also a hindrance to those around them who were truly seeking God.

A good biblical example of this is the parable found in Luke 18:10-14:

> *Two men went up into the temple to pray; the one a Pharisee, and
> the other a publican. The Pharisee stood and prayed thus with him-
> self, God, I thank thee, that I am not as other men are, extortioners,
> unjust, adulterers, or even as this publican. I fast twice in the week,
> I give tithes of all that I possess. And the publican, standing afar off,
> would not lift up so much as his eyes unto heaven, but smote upon*

NOTES

his breast, saying, God be merciful to me a sinner. I tell you, this man went down to his house justified rather than the other: for every one that exalteth himself shall be abased; and he that humbleth himself shall be exalted.

If we are not careful, we too will cross over that line. We will become spiritually proud. I have heard people praying who demand that God fulfill His word. The truth is that God's word is already fulfilled. If we do what God instructs us to do, we do not need to look to see if God is holding up His end of the bargain. God will do what He said He would do. Our attitude as we approach Step 7 should not be, "God, You said in Your Word that if I do this, then you would do that. Well, I have done what You have told me to do, so now You must do what You said You would do!" We cannot make God a debtor to His own Word. How arrogant is that?

Founder's Note 7, Step 7:

We also need to be careful about whom we are actually placing our trust in for salvation. If we are not careful, we will cross over that line between grace and works. We might sing with our lips, "My hope is built on nothing less than Jesus blood and righteousness," but as a friend so clearly pointed out to me, it is just as easy to sing a lie as to tell one. You might think you are trusting in Christ for your salvation, when in fact you are trusting in your own goodness. Jesus said to the church in Ephesus, *Nevertheless I have somewhat against thee, because thou hast left thy first love* (Revelation 2:4). We leave our first love when we become so enamored with what we are doing for God that it outweighs what God did for us. We should not ask God to change us because we want accolades from Him; instead, we need to ask God to change us because we are embarrassed and ashamed of the way we are.

Founder's Note 8, Step 7:

In Psalm 51, David makes the statement that his sin is ever before him. Many addicts would take exception to that statement, pointing out that God had forgiven David for his sins. Some addicts refuse to face the consequences of their sins. After all, hasn't God cast their sins as far away as the east is from the west? As addicts, we are always looking for the easy way out. We want to take the less painful approach to recovery. However, even though God could certainly deliver us by taking us out of a painful situation, it has been my experience that He will usually take us through it. If we can recognize the enormity of our sins, then in turn we will see and begin to understand the magnitude of God's amazing grace.

Not long ago, I was talking with my youngest daughter, Stephanie, and some things from the past came up in our conversation. At that point, I saw a shadow pass over my daughter's face. I knew that shadow was a painful memory that had resurfaced and was hurtful to her, even after all these years. The shadow was a painful reminder of an old wound I had previously inflicted on her. The knowledge that I had caused that pain overwhelmed me to the point that I felt

I was spinning out of control. You can steal more than a person's money; you can steal their childhood. How do you live with that? The only way I know to live with that is to walk in God's forgiveness.

When I am confronted with my sin, the only thing that keeps me putting one foot in front of the other, the only thing that keeps me moving ahead, is the knowledge that God, in His mercy and grace, has forgiven me. My friend Steve Gallagher wrote a Bible study entitled "Walk of Repentance." I think that if I had written that excellent study, I would have entitled it "Walk of Forgiveness." The truth is, we cannot circumvent the pain our choices have caused others, nor do I think God wants us to do that. By seeing our sins ever before us, we remain humble. In knowing that our sins have been forgiven, we remain grateful.

Founder's Note 9, Step 7:
In considering Ephesians 2:8-9 (page 80), the best advice I received when I was headed to prison for the first time was from an old convict who was getting out. We had met at the Justice Center in downtown Cleveland. He was being released, and I was in the process of receiving a two-year prison sentence. We both had hearings before the same judge, and while we were waiting, the old convict said to me, "You'll do all right in prison if you mind your own business, don't gamble, don't engage in homosexual activities, and never, ever forget where you are." The part about never, ever forgetting where you are is advice I share with my prison ministry volunteers today.

It is not just good to remember where we are, but we also need to remember where we were. To quote Jonathan Edwards, we were all "sinners in the hands of an angry God." John Newton described God's amazing grace when he wrote that God "saved a wretch like me." I believe it is true that we were all wretches when God saved us, because we were still in our sins. It is also true that once the blood of Christ has been applied to us, we are no longer wretches. Still, it is important for us to see that all of this is the result of God's actions and not our own. It is all about grace. Not only did God create within us the ability to believe, but He also gave us the object in which to place our beliefs – the person of Jesus Christ. We can take no credit for being delivered from our wretchedness. How, then, can we go before God with anything but a spirit of humility?

Founder's Note 10, Step 7:
A diagram that I often use is that of a stick man (I am not much of an artist) laboring up a steep mountain with a tremendous load on his back. That load is labeled as sin. Then I draw the same stick figure at the peak of the mountain in a joyful position, set free from sin by grace. Finally, I draw the stick figure in the future, laboring up the other side of the mountain with another tremendous bundle on his back labeled as works. It is important for the addict to realize that Christ died so that we could be set free.

NOTES

When I was released from prison the last time, one of my heart's secret desires was to meet Chuck Swindoll. Chuck Swindoll's ministry, Insight for Living, provided me with beautiful study guides and Bible studies which correlated to Swindoll's radio messages that I listened to nightly at 8:00 p.m. Dr. Swindoll's teachings were solid, and whenever he would recommend a particular book, like *Through Gates of Splendor* by Elisabeth Elliot, I made sure to read it. As a result, I grew in my understanding of God's Word, and I also grew in my faith. For six years, that ministry provided me with an evening Bible study that I could listen to five nights a week.

I remember one late December night having my little reading lamp on, listening to Chuck teach on Philemon. I glanced through the bars out into the prison yard where the ground was white with snow. I could see huge snowflakes falling. I began thinking of the Christmas carol, "Silent night, holy night, all is calm, all is bright." God's warmth and glow were very near to me that night, and I will never forget it. I thought that if I ever got out of prison, I would like to go meet Chuck Swindoll and personally thank him for this night and all the other nights I heard him preach and teach from the Word of God.

God knew I wanted to do this, so it was arranged for me to go to Texas. While there, I visited Stonebriar Church, where Chuck Swindoll is the senior pastor. Not only did I get to hear him preach, but I got to share a little of my testimony with him and express my gratitude for his ministry. Chuck Swindoll is a good man with no pretenses; what you see is what you get. He invited me to sit in the same section with him and his wife for all three services when he was preaching that morning! I was blessed as I listened to him preach the first sermon in a series of messages entitled "The Grace Awakening." The last thing he said to me as I was leaving stands out in my mind today. He said, "Larry, you know a lot more about what it means to be free than most people. Sell your freedom dearly."

This was a warning to me that some people within the church, within the body of Christ, will attempt to steal your freedom. It seems that once we understand that salvation is by faith, and we can do nothing to earn it, we fall into the trap of thinking we have to do something in order to keep it. Again, we are trying to put God in our debt. Cults thrive because they use salvation as a means to threaten people. There is no substitute for reading and knowing the Bible. It is all about grace!

Step 8

Restore

I have made a list of all the people my actions have or may have affected/damaged, and I ask myself, "How can I make this right?"

(Discuss each Bible verse by asking, "How does this particular verse apply to Step 8?")

Then it shall be, because he hath sinned, and is guilty, that he shall restore that which he took violently away, or the thing which he hath deceitfully gotten, or that which was delivered him to keep, or the lost thing which he found. (Leviticus 6:4)

Q. How would you define restitution?

If the wicked restore the pledge, give again that he had robbed, walk in the statutes of life, without committing iniquity; he shall surely live, he shall not die. None of his sins that he hath committed shall be mentioned unto him: he hath done that which is lawful and right; he shall surely live. (Ezekiel 33:15-16)

Q. How would you define rehabilitation?

Let him that stole steal no more: but rather let him labour, working with his hands the thing which is good, that he may have to give to him that needeth. (Ephesians 4:28)

Q. Does the Lord desire us to make restitution and to be rehabilitated?

Q. How would the two primary roots of addiction obstruct and even prevent us from making restitution or being rehabilitated?

Therefore if any man be in Christ, he is a new creature: old things are passed away; behold, all things are become new. (2 Corinthians 5:17)

Note: This is a wonderful promise from God, and we should not diminish or limit it in any way.

NOTES

This verse does not mean we are not going to have to deal with our past. What this verse promises is that we will see our past in a different light and face our problems in a new way.

Q. If all things become new and old things are passed away, why bother with this step at all?

Q. What really is new about Step 8?

Q. How can we make our wrongs right when we are unable or incapable of making those wrongs right?

Q. What are some ways we would be unable or incapable of redressing our wrongdoings?

Q. Will there still be present consequences for our past sins?

Q. What will be the major differences in the way we deal with these consequences?

Q. The Bible states in Exodus 20:12 that we are to honor our father and our mother. What does honor mean?

Note: We need to look at the whole concept of what it means to honor someone, and then we need to hold that concept in the light of what we are trying to accomplish in Step 8. When we honor people, we purpose in our hearts to do right by them. We resolve to give them a significant place in our lives. What they say, what they think, what they do, and how they feel matters to us. When we choose to honor people, people will honor us. The more people we choose to honor, the more enriched and full our lives will be.

Q. What does honoring people have to do with Step 8?

Q. How would honoring people help us to deal with the primary roots of addiction?

> *He hath shewed thee, O man, what is good; and what doth the Lord require of thee, but to do justly, and to love mercy, and to walk humbly with thy God?* (Micah 6:8)

Q. What does justly mean?

A. To do that which is right, fair, true, correct, and proper.

Q. One of the three requirements given to us in this verse is to do justly. How do you think this verse applies to Step 8?

Q. What are some ways we can do justly by the people we have wronged in the past?

Q. What are some ways we can do justly by the people who have wronged us in the past?

> *Therefore to him that knoweth to do good, and doeth it not, to him it is sin.* (James 4:17)

Q. How does this verse in James apply to our goals in Step 8?

Q. What is the warning here if we do not try to make things right?

> *Therefore if thou bring thy gift to the altar, and there rememberest that thy brother hath ought against thee; leave there thy gift before the altar, and go thy way; first be reconciled to thy brother, and then come and offer thy gift.* (Matthew 5:23-24)

Review: Reconciled means to become friendly again or to settle a quarrel or dispute.

Q. Who do we need to reconcile with first and foremost?

Q. How do we achieve reconciliation with God?

Q. How do you think being right with God helps us to be right with others?

Note: Surely God wants us to right our wrongs whenever possible. However, in many instances, we may find this difficult to do. People may not want to hear from us or see us. People may have died or moved, and we may have no idea where they are or how to contact them. People may even have put restraining orders against us, preventing us from contacting them. In this case, we must not contact them under any circumstances! An old adage which may apply here is, "Old wounds are better left alone." This means that by trying to undo something, we might actually be making it worse. Psalm 37 tells us that God gives us the desires of our heart if we delight ourselves in Him. God also knows when we have the desire in our hearts to make things right with others. God will bless that desire and He will do for us what we cannot do for ourselves. What we are unable to do, we give to God and trust Him to make it right. The key is to ask for God's help in doing what we can and trust Him with the rest.

Q. How should we deal with those who have wronged us?

> *Say not thou, I will recompense evil; but wait on the LORD, and he shall save thee.* (Proverbs 20:22)

NOTES

Q. What does recompense mean?

A. To repay or to compensate for.[12]

Q. What does it mean to wait on the Lord?

Q. What is the Lord saving us from in Proverbs 20:22?

Q. What is our natural reaction (as a result of our sinful nature) to someone injuring us?

Q. What are some ways we have responded in the past to someone who has injured us either physically, emotionally, or mentally?

Note: Now we address the flip side of Step 8 in a biblical manner. What do we do about those who have sinned against us in the past? First, we need to determine if it was our own actions that caused these people to sin against us. Were they reacting to something we did to them or to someone they love? If so, then we must place the blame where it belongs – on ourselves. What about those people whom we ask to forgive us, but they refuse to do so? Who was it that caused their reaction to our plea for forgiveness? Again, we need to lay the blame on ourselves. If we would not have damaged them in the first place, we would not need to ask their forgiveness.

What about those people who have hurt us in the past and we were not responsible for that hurt? Perhaps we were molested as children, or maybe our parents were addicts. How should we respond in these instances? (Discuss)

And when ye stand praying, forgive, if ye have ought against any: that your Father also which is in heaven may forgive you your trespasses. (Mark 11:25)

Note: The clue to dealing with those who have sinned against us is to fully understand how God dealt with us for those sins we committed against Him. We who have received grace, mercy, and forgiveness from God need to be able to extend the same to others. Ephesians 4:32 says *And be ye kind one to another, tenderhearted, forgiving one another, even as God for Christ's sake hath forgiven you.*

Q. Are there people in your past whom you are having trouble forgiving?

Q. If so, are you willing to discuss this with the group?

Who is a God like unto thee, that pardoneth iniquity, and passeth by the transgression of the remnant of his heritage? He retaineth not his anger forever, because he delighteth in mercy. He will turn again,

12   http://www.dictionary.com/browse/recompense.

he will have compassion upon us; he will subdue our iniquities; and thou wilt cast all their sins into the depths of the sea. (Micah 7:18-19)

Q. Is God willing to forgive our wrongdoing?

Q. Once our sins are forgiven, does God hold them against us?

Q. If God loves mercy, shouldn't we love mercy? (See Micah 6:8)

Q. If God is willing to forgive us, shouldn't we be willing to forgive others?

Then came Peter to him, and said, Lord, how oft shall my brother sin against me, and I forgive him? till seven times? Jesus saith unto him, I say not unto thee, Until seven times: but, Until seventy times seven. (Matthew 18:21-22)

Q. What do you think Jesus meant by seventy times seven? (Discuss)

Read and discuss Matthew 18:23-35.

And all things are of God, who hath reconciled us to himself by Jesus Christ, and hath given to us the ministry of reconciliation; to wit, that God was in Christ, reconciling the world unto himself, not imputing their trespasses unto them; and hath committed unto us the word of reconciliation. (2 Corinthians 5:18-19)

Q. How has God given us a ministry of reconciliation?

Q. What is another name for the word of reconciliation?

A. The gospel according to the Scriptures.

Write down your own thoughts about Step 8. If you make a list, you may dispose of it. It is not necessary for anyone but you to know what is on that list. However, I want you to consider the ripple effects of your actions.

As addicts, we tend to minimize the consequences of our actions, so please put some thought and effort into this. Do not be so quick to excuse what you have done. Think it through all the way to the consequences, and if you do, it will help you deal with and overcome not only your addictions but your past as well. Keep it real.

Founder's Notes with Illustrations Step 8

Step 8 - <u>Restore</u>: I have made a list of all the people my actions have or may have affected/damaged, and I ask myself, "How can I make this right?"

Founder's Note 1, Step 8:

It is important to note here that a person is usually on fire for the Lord after being born again. How that fire is directed and contained can make or break a new Christian. When I was selling cars, we would go to breakfast meetings and listen to motivational speakers. When I left those meetings, I would be fired up. I would determine in my mind that I was going to sell a car to the first customer who had the audacity to show up on our car lot.

I remember one such instance when a middle-aged couple stopped by to shop after I had just finished one of those morning motivational meetings. I was loaded for bear. I asked all the right qualifying questions. We were taught to avoid questions that a customer could simply answer with a yes or no. For example, the correct question would be: "Are you looking for a new car or for a used car?" or "Would you like a four-door or a two-door car?" Having qualified the couple, I then took the lead, just as the motivational speaker had instructed. With all the authority I could muster, I said, "Follow me!" and as directed, I didn't look back. I just led the way, knowing they would follow, because that is what the speaker had said the customers would do.

When I got to the car that I thought I could sell them, I looked around, and to my dismay they had not followed me at all; instead, they had gone their own way, and another salesperson had picked them up! This truly put a leak in my artificial balloon. I was so deflated that it affected my sales in a negative way for the rest of the month.

A cautious approach to Step 8 is the best approach. Some people will not want to hear from us again. Some people will never forgive us for the things we have done. You cannot make someone forgive you, nor should you be indignant when they do not. That would be a result of pride, maybe even wounded pride. We must remember that those whom we have hurt are not to blame. Our past actions caused this result.

People who are still living a worldly life will not understand what it means to be born again; therefore, they cannot comprehend the change that is taking place within us. We need to go slowly and ask God to place upon our hearts those things He would have us do. If you are not careful, you will fire out of the starting gate only to hit a brick wall, resulting in your resolve to complete this step, dampened or totally destroyed. You may even grow disillusioned with your Christian walk.

Founder's Note 2, Step 8:

When we do the right thing, right things will happen. However, they may not happen right away. We may have to apologize several times over a long period of time before someone accepts our apology. Our initial "I'm sorry" may be met with a profane rebuff. This can be discouraging, especially if we were anticipating a favorable response or a positive reply. The Bible states that we are never to tire of doing good, which in my mind prompts the question, "Why would anyone ever tire of doing what is good?" The answer is that we are viewed by others as having ulterior motives for our actions. In other words, people think that we are up to something. Why wouldn't they? We *are* up to something! The truth is, that is the only reason we did any good deed in the past. When we seek to make things right, we should do so without any thought of reward or a desire for people to like us. We should not do it to try to feel good about ourselves. We should want to make things right out of a genuine desire to do so in the eyes of God. While attempting to work this step, we must always ask ourselves why we are doing what we are doing.

Founder's Note 3, Step 8:

To illustrate that our motivation is important, I will give a worldly example of which I am personally ashamed. December is usually a hard month for those who sell cars. Sales are usually slow, but one year I was having an unusually good December, while my friend was having an unusually bad one. We both worked for straight commission. My friend had a large family, and I knew he would be hard-pressed to buy Christmas presents for his children or to even put groceries on their table. I had just begun dating an uptown girl at that time, and I was looking for ways to make a good impression on her, so what did I do? I bought groceries and presents for my friend and his family, but I made sure to take my new girlfriend along. When I knocked on my friend's door, he smiled when he saw me, and I could see the look of gratitude on his face when he saw the groceries and gifts I had brought. Then he saw the girl behind me, and his face dropped. He knew exactly what my motivation was for being there, and it was not to help him or his family. I will never forget that look on his face. I made a good impression on the girl, but I lost a friend and gained a memory that to this day I wish I could erase.

Founder's Note 4, Step 8:

I mentioned in the workbook section for this step (page 91) that sometimes we have restraining orders against us. It bears repeating that in no way should we violate a restraining order, even if our reasons for doing so are to make things right. I can guarantee that your judge or parole officer will not understand or care about your motivation. We are to obey the law. If we live a Christ-centered life and allow God to make the repairs in the order He wishes, then we will never be disappointed with the results. When I was released from prison, I did not force myself back on my family; instead, I prayed, "Lord if You give my family back to me, I will praise You: but if You don't give my family back to me, I will still praise You. This is what my life is all about – praising You."

I heard Chuck Swindoll say on one of his radio broadcasts, "If it flows, it's from God, and if it's forced, it's from me." I do not want to kick a door open; I want God to open the door for me. It took a long time for me to inflict all the damage I inflicted on people, and it will take a long time to repair the damage. I need to be sensitive to that still small voice that speaks to me, saying, "This is the way, walk in it."

Founder's Note 5, Step 8:

Our parole officer, the judge, and those in authority over us are not the enemy. We view them as such because they are a threat to our ability to retain our addictions. They seek to take away those things that we addicts refer to as triggers. Those in authority seek to prevent us from using, and therefore we despise them because we view them as a threat. The truth is, as long as we view them this way, we are a threat to ourselves and to others. Prideful people cannot submit themselves to authority, nor can they stand reproof. The thing that angered me most when I was a drunk was when someone called me a drunk. Why? It was because I was trying to keep that part of myself hidden. We do not want to be discovered, because if we are, we may have to give up our addictions. Instead, we get angry. In our prideful condition, we resent the very people who are trying to help us.

Founder's Note 6, Step 8:

Part of Step 8 is seeing our need to forgive those who have wrongfully abused us. Every now and then in prison we would be faced with a guard who abused his or her power. Maybe this person had never been in a position of authority before. Maybe the guard was just taking out on us what he had been unable to take out on his spouse or his children at home. Whatever the reason, the guards sometimes would become abusive and severe in their attitudes toward us inmates. In other words, they were looking to pick a fight.

Before I was saved, I would get angry with this type of guard, but after I was born again, I realized my actions had placed me where these abusive people were in a position of authority over me, and I began to put the blame squarely on the person who deserved it – me. If I needed to be angry at someone, that someone was me. I began to pray for those people who were so miserable that they felt a need to take out their misery on others.

Founder's Note 7, Step 8:

We will never know the full extent of the damage our choices and actions have caused. For example, when I deliver Angel Tree presents to kids whose parents are incarcerated, I see that many times the grandparents are raising the kids. God never intended for grandparents to be raising children. Raising children puts a physical strain on older people who are already beginning to experience the physical strains of old age. They tire much more quickly than they used to, and it is hard for them to get down on the floor and play. It is difficult for them to go out and toss a ball around; sometimes it's even hard for them to lift a child.

The mental strain on older people is greater, too. Older people are looking for a little peace and quiet, while kids are looking for just the opposite. Children want to do, do, do, and older people want to sit. It is also a financial strain on the grandparents, and one I am sure they did not consider when they were planning for old age. So, instead of traveling and enjoying their golden years, they are raising their children's children. Most senior adults have fixed incomes, and this puts a strain on the budget, which in turn can lead to spouses arguing with one another, putting a strain on their relationship. If they are living in a strained relationship at home, chances are relationships outside the home will become strained as well.

It goes on and on. I call it the ripple effect. This is the example that I use when I am trying to encourage addicts to face the full consequences of their choices. I am just beginning to scratch the surface, and in a group session, you can certainly add to it or think of your own examples. This is a very important discussion, because it makes us look at the full consequences of our actions. When we begin to see the full magnitude of our sins, we begin to understand how great God's mercy is to forgive us of our sins. The greater our understanding of the full extent of God's forgiveness toward us, the more forgiving and tolerant we will be of others.

Founder's Note 8, Step 8:

In Step 8, we are asked to make a list of all the people our actions have affected or damaged. This will inevitably bring up the question, "What about people who have hurt me in the past?" This question should not be avoided but should be addressed at this point. While working with inmates, I have heard stories of child abuse so horrible that it is beyond my understanding. Some people will demonstrate a need for additional help and counseling beyond that which we can offer. As addicts taking part in this program, we must not be afraid to admit when we come up against things that are more than we can handle. It is okay to admit that we need help. Program or step leaders should never be afraid to admit that some people's problems are beyond their capability to understand.

I think we would all agree that people who molest children are guilty of some of the most heinous crimes in our society. Yet, according to psychologists, many of these people were themselves abused as children. This certainly doesn't excuse their actions as adults. Two wrongs can never make a right, but it does point out the need to understand our past and forgive those who have wronged us. If we do not forgive those who have wrongfully abused us, we allow those individuals to continue to affect us in a negative way. In a sense, the abuse is ongoing. We could even, over a period of time, become like them. By seeing our need to be forgiven, we will see our need to forgive. We will then step out of the past and into the present, free at last.

Founder's Note 9, Step 8:

As addicts, we use crutches such as shifting blame, minimizing, or rationalization. We need to train ourselves to be aware of the presence of those things when we are making our list and evaluating the full extent of the damage we have caused others. I once had an inmate come up to me after class and begin what I would refer to as a suck-up conversation. All he needed was an apple to present to the teacher. During that discussion, he mentioned that he was in prison for having sex with an underage girl. I asked him how old the girl was, and he said that she was twelve. I looked that man squarely in the eyes and said, "Before we go any further in this conversation, you need to understand something. You are not in prison for having sex with an underage girl; you are in prison for raping a baby! There is a little girl somewhere who is sleeping with her light on because of you."

I was not judging the man; I was trying to make him see and come to grips with the terrible thing he had done. As a program facilitator (or even as members who are accountable to one another), we need to listen to others and confront them either one-on-one or in front of the group when they attempt to minimize their actions. Minimization is exactly what we are trying to avoid here! When Step 8 is approached with the proper attitude and with the intent of getting to the heart of the problem no matter how painful the results are, those results can be life changing. I have seen many people broken as they work through this step. The key is to be able to see the consequences of what we have done, and if we can do that when we are faced with a similar choice or choices, we will make the right decision. We will consider the cost and will choose not to act out.

Founder's Note 10, Step 8:

There is a flip side to Step 8. This step encourages us to humble ourselves before others. We feel good when we say, "I'm sorry" and actually mean it. We feel good when someone accepts our apology. As addicts, we find it difficult to admit to others that we are wrong. We would prefer to run away and hide from someone rather than apologize to that person. We are always looking for a shortcut, trying to save ourselves from pain and embarrassment. I had a prison chaplain tell me once that embarrassment is the pennant that flies over the castle of pride. This step is a great tenderizer of the heart.

Founder's Note 11, Step 8:

I owed a great deal of child support when I got out of prison. When I called the Bureau of Support, the lady with whom I spoke was amazed at the amount. She asked me why I was not in prison since I owed so much. I told her that the reason I owed so much was because I had been in prison. She informed me that due to my circumstances, I could probably complete some paperwork which could possibly result in the amount I owed being reduced. I said I did not want to do that. She was flabbergasted to say the least. When she asked me why, my reply was, "I owe the money and I want to pay the full amount." I said, "I want my kids to know they have a father." A lot of good things have happened in my family relationships because I made that decision. That was not why I made that decision though. I made that decision because I wanted to do the right thing before God. I did not look for the easy way out but looked for the right way out. I have never regretted that decision. God will honor a decision made from a heart that is seeking to do the right thing.

Step 9

Pursue

> **D**aily, I seek to know and live out God's will, plan, and purpose for my life.

(Discuss each Bible verse by asking, "How does this particular verse apply to Step 9?")

Note: If you have given your life to Christ, you will be changed. The change starts slowly, but you will find yourself acting and reacting to situations differently from the way you had responded to similar situations in the past. Maybe you have already noticed some changes. Share with the group (voluntarily) some of the changes you have noticed about yourself. Have other people noticed the changes in you? (Discuss)

> *The fear of the Lord is the beginning of wisdom: and the knowledge of the holy is understanding.* (Proverbs 9:10)

Note: Knowing that God exists and coming to an understanding that He is holy will result in the realization that we are not holy and can never be holy without God's help. This is the foundation of seeing the need to change from someone who is self-centered to someone who is God-centered.

Q. What do you think the meaning of fear is in the above verse? (Review the worksheet and Ephesians 5:21.)

> *But seek ye first the kingdom of God, and his righteousness; and all these things shall be added unto you.* (Matthew 6:33)

Note: The kingdom of God is found in the person of Jesus Christ. If we receive Him as our Lord and Savior, we have this new nature; we are to seek God's will first and foremost. Then *all these things*, the desires of our regenerated heart, will come to fruition.

Q. How do we receive the righteousness of God? (Read 1 Corinthians 1:30 and discuss.)

Q. What does all these things mean to you?

NOTES

But as it is written, Eye hath not seen, nor ear heard, neither have entered into the heart of man, the things which God hath prepared for them that love him. (1 Corinthians 2:9)

Note: This is a promise from God. He has a will, a plan, and a purpose for our lives. God wants to turn us into something beautiful. The things He has purposed for us are so wondrous that we cannot even begin to imagine them.

Q. What is our part in fulfilling this promise from God?

Q. Do you think God will keep this promise? If so, what is keeping you from living it out?

Review:

In Step 9 we acknowledge that God has a will, a plan, and a purpose for our lives. God's will is perfect. Our will is flawed and steeped in pride and self-centeredness. We now begin to chart a new course, but first, let us define God's will, plan, and purpose for our lives and agree on what it is.

Q. What is God's will for our lives?

A. God's will for our lives is that we are restored to a right relationship with Him through the blood of His Son and we receive eternal life.

For I know the thoughts that I think toward you, saith the Lord, thoughts of peace, and not of evil, to give you an expected end. (Jeremiah 29:11)

Note: Many teach this as part of a prosperity doctrine, but in reality it is talking about restoration. We have all purposely sinned against God. We have rebelled against Him in every way imaginable. We have lived our lives excluding God as if He did not exist. Despite all our rebellion, God, who has the right and the might to punish us, is not thinking about that. He is thinking about restoring us to a right relationship with Him. His gift to us is eternal life through Christ, and our expected end is to reign with Him in glory. Jeremiah 29:11 is a salvation verse. God wants you to be saved.

Q. In view of the above, what do you think thoughts of peace, and not of evil means?

For I have no pleasure in the death of him that dieth, saith the Lord God: wherefore turn yourselves, and live ye. (Ezekiel 18:32)

Q. Does God take pleasure in punishing us?

Q. Whose choice is it whether we live or die?

> *For God sent not his Son into the world to condemn the world; but that the world through him might be saved.* (John 3:17)

Q. Did Christ come into the world to judge the world?

Q. What does it mean to be saved?

Q. Is the body of Christ in the world to judge the world?

A. No. The body of Christ is in the world to draw others to Christ that they might be saved.

Q. Why did God send His Son into the world?

Q. How do we become saved?

> *The Lord is not slack concerning his promise, as some men count slackness; but is longsuffering to us-ward, not willing that any should perish, but that all should come to repentance.* (2 Peter 3:9)

Note: There will come a time when God will say it is over, and we will be sealed in the decision we have made concerning His Son. Today, we are in a period of grace. God is allowing us time to repent and come to the saving knowledge of Christ.

Q. Can you repent and not be saved? (Discuss)

Note: Longsuffering means we have been wronged and therefore have the right to retaliate, but choose instead to allow the person(s) who wronged us time to apologize or make things right.

Q. Is longsuffering the same as patience?

> *It is of the Lord's mercies that we are not consumed, because his compassions fail not. They are new every morning: great is thy faithfulness.* (Lamentations 3:22-23)

> *Who will have all men to be saved, and to come unto the knowledge of the truth.* (1 Timothy 2:4)

> *Who gave himself for our sins, that he might deliver us from this present evil world, according to the will of God and our Father.* (Galatians 1:4)

NOTES

_____
_____
_____
_____
_____
_____
_____
_____
_____
_____
_____
_____
_____
_____
_____
_____
_____
_____

According to the above three verses:

Q. What is God's will for all mankind?

Q. Who is the truth?

> *And this is the Father's will which hath sent me, that of all which he hath given me I should lose nothing, but should raise it up again at the last day.* (John 6:39)

Note: When we give our lives to Christ, He will not lose us or let us go. The same power that raised Jesus from the grave will raise us from the grave. What a wonderful promise! In order to truly understand this promise, we must understand how the Holy Trinity works in one accord toward our salvation. We are drawn to the Son by the Father. The Father is not going to draw people who have not been reproved by the Holy Spirit and convicted of their unbelief. No man comes to the Father unless it is through the Son. Note the following three verses:

> *Jesus saith unto him, I am the way, the truth, and the life: no man cometh unto the Father, but by me.* (John 14:6)

> *No man can come to me, except the Father which hath sent me draw him: and I will raise him up at the last day.* (John 6:44)

> *And when he is come, he will reprove the world of sin, and of righteousness, and of judgment: of sin, because they believe not on me.* (John 16:8-9)

Note: God wants all people to be saved, and salvation is truly the work of the Lord. We complete God's will for our lives when we give our lives to Christ. Once saved, we, too, as the body of Christ, enter into God's work. Our lives take on a new purpose, and that is to see others saved, for this is the will of God. Once we are saved and receive a new nature, the nature of Christ, God's will and our will become one.

Q. What is God's plan for our lives?

A. We are to make His Son known to a lost and dying generation.

> *There was a man sent from God, whose name was John. The same came for a witness, to bear witness of the Light, that all men through him might believe. He was not that Light, but was sent to bear witness of that Light.* (John 1:6-8)

Q. To which John are we referring here?

Q. Who is the Light?

Q. What was God's plan for John the Baptist?

Q. What is God's plan for us?

Note: God's methods never change. Whether He is dealing with an individual, a nation, or on a universal plane, His methods remain the same. *I am the LORD, I change not* (Malachi 3:6).

> *For we are his workmanship, created in Christ Jesus unto good*
> *works, which God hath before ordained that we should walk in them.*
> (Ephesians 2:10)

Q. Whose workmanship are we?

Q. Can you name some of the good works God has called His people to do?

Note: God's plan to redeem fallen man was *before ordained*. This simply means that God's plan for us to be saved and to bear witness of His Son was in place long before man chose to sin.

Q. Do you think it is possible that we could do something that surprises God in such a way that He is unprepared for the outcome?

> *But ye are a chosen generation, a royal priesthood, an holy nation, a*
> *peculiar people; that ye should shew forth the praises of him who hath*
> *called you out of darkness into his marvellous light.* (1 Peter 2:9)

Note: This is what church people refer to as a calling. We are the generation being called upon today. How will our generation shine compared to past generations? This is our time to shine for Jesus. How we shine for Jesus today will glow throughout eternity and help to light the way for generations that follow. It is exciting to know that God's plan for us has eternal worth.

Q. What does peculiar mean?

A. Distinctive in nature or character from others.[13]

Q. What makes us a peculiar people?

> *Holding forth the word of life; that I may rejoice in the day of*
> *Christ, that I have not run in vain, neither laboured in vain.*
> (Philippians 2:16)

---

13   *http://www.dictionary.com/browse/peculiar?s=t.*

NOTES

Note: Our calling is to be holding forth the Word of life to those who are perishing. Everything that I think, do, and say should be done with the purpose of drawing others to Christ. If what I think, do, or say is done for any other reason than drawing others to the Lord out of love for the Lord, it is done in vain.

Q. What does in vain mean?

Q. What does vanity mean and how is it related to pride?

Verily, verily, I say unto you, He that believeth on me, the works that I do shall he do also; and greater works than these shall he do; because I go unto my Father. (John 14:12)

Q. Who is being quoted in this verse?

Q. What are some of the miracles that Jesus performed while He was here on earth?

Q. How could we possibly do greater works than Jesus did?

Q. How are we empowered to do greater works than these?

Q. What are the two conditional statements in John 14:12?

A. He that believeth on me and because I go unto my Father.

Q. How can Jesus going to His Father enable us to fulfill this verse?

Note: This is one of the most exciting verses in the Bible. The God who created the cosmos is talking about us doing great works. When Jesus is talking about greater works, it is from God's perspective, not our own. God's ways are higher than our ways, and the greater works Jesus is envisioning are far greater than anything we could ever imagine. When you share the gospel with someone and that person believes and receives it, a deaf person has finally heard, a blind person can see, and someone who was dead in his trespasses now lives forever and will reign with God in glory. That is our calling. That is God's plan for us. Could there be anything greater than that?

Let him know, that he which converteth the sinner from the error of his way shall save a soul from death, and shall hide a multitude of sins. (James 5:20)

Q. How can a sinner's soul be saved and his sins hidden?

And ye also shall bear witness, because ye have been with me from the beginning. (John 15:27)

Q. How could we have been with Christ since the beginning?

A. We have been fully restored and justified, born again from the beginning.

Q. What is God's purpose for our lives?

A. That we glorify Him through Christ.

Note: Now we enter the third and final phase of Step 9 by asking ourselves, "What is God's purpose for our lives?"

This spake he, signifying by what death he should glorify God. And when he had spoken this, he saith unto him, Follow me. (John 21:19)

Q. What death was Jesus speaking about?

Q. How did that death glorify God?

Q. How are we to respond to the death of Jesus on the cross?

I am crucified with Christ: nevertheless I live; yet not I, but Christ liveth in me: and the life which I now live in the flesh I live by the faith of the Son of God, who loved me, and gave himself for me. (Galatians 2:20)

Note: When we are baptized, we are publicly acknowledging that we have taken part in the death, burial, and resurrection of Jesus.

Q. What does it mean to be crucified with Christ?

Q. What should our response be to the One who gave Himself over to death so that we might live?

A. We give Him all the praise and glory for saving us, changing our lives, and setting us free.

And call upon me in the day of trouble: I will deliver thee, and thou shalt glorify me. (Psalm 50:15)

Note: Everyone has a day of trouble, and how we respond on that day determines where we will spend eternity. If we turn to God, we will be delivered. As a result of that deliverance, we realize that we could not have saved ourselves,

NOTES

but instead had to be saved. We also realize that only God could have saved us. We give God the glory for our salvation, and out of our grateful hearts, we live to glorify Him. We were lost, but now we are found. Our lives were without hope and without purpose. We now have a sure hope, and our lives are filled with purpose. To God be the glory, great things He hath done.

> *I will praise thee, O Lord my God, with all my heart: and I will glorify thy name for evermore.* (Psalm 86:12)

Note: This is the attitude of gratitude we need to develop. If you have gone more than ten minutes without thanking God for something, you have gone too long.

> *Let your light so shine before men, that they may see your good works, and glorify your Father which is in heaven.* (Matthew 5:16)

Q. What is meant here by good works?

Q. When we do good works, who is actually doing those good works?

Q. Who should get the glory for those good works?

> *That ye may with one mind and one mouth glorify God, even the Father of our Lord Jesus Christ. Wherefore receive ye one another, as Christ also received us to the glory of God.* (Romans 15:6-7)

Q. As the body of Christ, we are to be of one accord in our praise of God. Do you think that is true of God's people today? Are we of one accord? If not, why not?

Q. We are to receive one another as Christ received us. What condition were we in when Christ received us?

Q. How has pride and self-centeredness affected the body of Christ today?

Review Galatians 5:19, which presents a list of the works of the flesh. Are these works evident in the church today? (Discuss)

> *He shall glorify me: for he shall receive of mine, and shall shew it unto you.* (John 16:14)

Q. Who is Jesus speaking of here?

A. The Holy Spirit

> *I have sworn by myself, the word is gone out of my mouth in*

*righteousness, and shall not return, that unto me every knee shall
bow, every tongue shall swear.* (Isaiah 45:23)

Q. This verse in Isaiah is prophetic and messianic. What or who is the word
mentioned in the verse above?

In the LORD shall all the seed of Israel be justified, and shall glory.
(Isaiah 45:25)

Q. Who is the seed of Israel today?

Note: Our glory has never been in and of ourselves. If we were true addicts, we
had nothing left to lose. We lived a life that shamed us and those who loved
us. Today, if we have given our lives over to Christ, if we have been born again,
then His glory is now our glory, and His Father calls us His friend. It is not who
we are, but who we are in Christ that makes all the difference. You will never
be able to make a better decision than that. If you have not made a decision to
receive Christ, won't you please do it now?

*For it is written, As I live, saith the Lord, every knee shall bow to me,
and every tongue shall confess to God.* (Romans 14:11)

*That at the name of Jesus every knee should bow, of things in heaven,
and things in earth, and things under the earth; and that every
tongue should confess that Jesus Christ is Lord, to the glory of God
the Father.* (Philippians 2:10-11)

Q. What is the end result of Christ's work on the cross?

Q. What tools do we have as Christians to accomplish God's will, God's plan,
and God's purpose for our lives? (Discuss)

Founder's Notes with Illustrations for Step 9

**Step 9 – <u>Pursue</u>: Daily, I seek to know and live out God's will, plan,
and purpose for my life.**

Founder's Note 1, Step 9:

A story is told about a frog who lived in a well. The well was the only world
that the frog had ever known. One day, the frog in the well looked up and saw
another frog sitting on the lip of the well. The frog on the lip began to tell the
frog in the well about all the things that were in the world outside the well. The
frog in the well couldn't believe the things he was hearing, and he accused the

NOTES

_____

_____

_____

_____

_____

_____

_____

_____

_____

_____

_____

_____

_____

_____

_____

_____

_____

_____

other frog of not being truthful. The frog on the lip said, "Jump up here and follow me, and I'll prove to you that everything I have told you is true." So the frog in the well jumped up to the lip, out onto the grass, and hopped with the other frog up a steep hillside. When they reached the top of the hill, the vast expanse of the ocean lay beneath them. At this point, the head of the frog from the well exploded. He could not handle that much knowledge that fast. That would also be true for us if God decided to download to our brains the minutest portion of everything He knows.

God gives us what we can handle when He deems we can handle it. We may want everything now, but God knows we cannot handle it. We would go insane; our heads would explode. While teaching from the book of Ephesians, Chuck Swindoll said that "anyone who could understand the totality of this book is the fourth person of the Godhead." Some things are mysteries and will continue to be mysteries until the time that God reveals them to us. However, God does have a will, a plan, and a purpose for my life. He will reveal those things to me. He will not keep those things a mystery.

Founder's Note 2, Step 9:

No matter what circumstances we were born into, we can rise above them. Life is not always fair, but God has a purpose for each and every one of us. One night I was coming home from the Trumbull Correctional Institution near Youngstown, Ohio, and I decided to stop at a diner. As I got out of my car, I saw an older man and a younger man going inside. They went in just ahead of me, and the waitress happened to seat me in a booth where I could hear their conversation. These two men were father and son. Apparently, the son was beginning his freshman year at college and wanted to live with a bunch of other male students in one of those large multi-room off-campus houses. The college must have been close to the young man's home, because the father asked his son not to move out until after his sophomore year.

However, it was the way the father asked that amazed me. He told his son that whatever he decided, they (he and his wife) would accept. He went on to explain how years ago when he had attended college, he had made the same decision his son was now contemplating, but many of his "friends" had left, sticking him with the bills. He had been forced to take a second job to pay off what was owed. He explained that if he had not done that, his credit would have been ruined, and it would have kept them from ever living in the nice house they owned today. He told his son that they wanted him to get a good start in college. Then he made a counteroffer. The father told his son that they would make him an apartment in the basement with his own entry/exit door and driveway. He promised that neither he nor the young man's mother would police their son's coming and going. They would give him absolute privacy. "The decision is yours to make," the father said, "and your mother and I will honor that decision."

Wow! No one had ever spoken to me in such a way. My parents did the best they could for me, but never did I receive anything near this type of discussion from them about school or anything else for that matter. We cannot choose the circumstances into which we are born. We cannot choose our parents, nor can they choose their children.

As addicts, most of us were not born into a *Leave-it-to-Beaver* household. For those of you who do not remember *Leave it to Beaver*, the Cleavers (*Beaver* was Theodore Cleaver's nickname) were the ideal family. Mom always wore a dress and makeup, and her hair was perfect. Dad wore a tie and suitcoat or sweater, except on Saturdays. The family always ate dinner together and engaged in lengthy conversations during their meals. I could go on, but I'm sure you get the picture. I remember the first Christian couple I met while I was in prison. They would come every Tuesday night and teach a Bible study. The way they were raising their children was totally different from the way I was raised. Addicts often grow up in broken homes or as latchkey kids, but that is not always the case.

What we need to remember is that we all have a perfect Father in heaven. We all have a Christian family. God provides that for us. He levels the playing field. No matter the conditions in which we were raised or the environment in which we grew up, we need to get over the past and on with the present.

Founder's Note 3, Step 9:

After visiting a prison near Atmore, Alabama, one January night, I returned to the room where I was staying. Deciding to watch some television, I did some channel surfing, but found nothing I really wanted to see. For whatever reason, I began to watch some men playing a card game called Texas Hold'em. I had not played much poker, but I knew the basics of the game. I was amazed to see players repeatedly throw in the best hand after another player bluffed them. I began to realize you could win with any hand you are dealt in poker. I think the same is true in life. It is all a matter of attitude and perspective. And even better than poker, each Christian wins. There are no losers in the kingdom of God.

Founder's Note 4, Step 9:

I love to tell men and women in prison that they do not have to go another day as a loser. In Christ, they, too, can experience victory. The same is true for those who are locked in the prisons of addiction. There is a way out. Jesus said, "I am the way."

Founder's Note 5, Step 9:

After preaching at a Baptist church in Letterkenny, Ireland, a deacon invited me and the rest of the congregation to have lunch at his house. When I arrived at the deacon's house, I noticed a tent and several large grills where some great-looking food was cooking. (Baptists around the world have many things in common, not the least of which is that we all like to eat. Sometimes I think a good Baptist pennant would be a flag with a picture of a Bible, a cross, and a fork. No offense is meant here, and I pray none is taken.)

While I was eating, a young lady sat down next to me and told me her story. She said she was from Holland and was attending a local college for nursing. She had been in a federal prison in Atlanta, Georgia, for three years for smuggling drugs from Holland to the United States. During her time in prison, she had been confined to a two-person cell. Her cellmate was a lady who had been sentenced to life without the possibility of parole, but who had been born again. The young nursing student told me how her cellmate would pray for her during the day and that she "was always trying to show me something out of her Bible. I hated her because of that," the young lady told me.

By the way, be prepared not to expect a hug or a kiss on the cheek when you tell someone about Jesus. Matthew Henry said that the Word of God irritates the carnal mind, and I want to tell you that the name of Jesus does the same. You can bring up the names of the most heinous people in history and not get the reaction you will get when you mention the name of Jesus. We need to be prepared for that, but we need to mention Him anyway, because that is God's plan for our lives.

The nursing student went on to tell me that two days before she was released from prison, her cellmate led her to the Lord. Now she wanted to lead others to Jesus, so she had brought two guests to the church service that day – two Hindu ladies who were her classmates at the nurse's college and had never attended a Christian service before. Again, God's plan for our lives is to introduce others to Jesus.

When sharing with inmates, one thing I bring up is that the time they spend locked up does not have to be wasted. I tell them that God will use them where they are. The cellmate of that nursing student in Ireland is serving a life sentence. Most would say that her life is a waste; however, this is not the case, because that lady doing life in prison has a ministry in Ireland! We were created to glorify God and have fellowship with Him. We can do that wherever we are.

Founder's Note 6, Step 9:

When I discuss longsuffering, I use an illustration from my past. I am not proud of what happened, but we can learn from it. I have found that I can use secular events to make a biblical application. When I went to bars and drank on Friday nights, I was not opposed to picking a fight every now and again. I was careful, though, with whom I picked a fight. I would always scan the bar and pick on a person I thought I could beat, but not someone too small. It was ok with me if I had an edge by fighting a person smaller than myself, but not so small that others would think I was a bully.

One Friday night I decided to pick a fight with the man seated on the barstool next to me. He looked rather short and thin, like someone I could beat. I verbally assaulted this fellow. My words struck a nerve with him, and he got up off his stool. There have been times in my life, and I'm sure in yours, when things are said or done that we immediately regret. This was one of those times. I watched as the man stood up, and to my dismay he seemed to grow taller and taller. He was one of those individuals who had a short trunk but long legs. I also saw that he was not thin but was lean and wiry. Unfortunately, this man was not longsuffering. He gave me the licking of my life that night, and to this day I wish I had not picked that fight. If you think about it, we have been provoking

God into a fight all our lives. He certainly is in the right and He certainly has the might to retaliate. Instead, He waits for us to apologize, and then He forgives us. Amazing grace!

Founder's Note 7, Step 9:

G. Campbell Morgan, my favorite Bible expositor, wrote in *The Gospel According to John* that we are to be salt. He wrote that salt is aseptic and not antiseptic. That means salt will not cure infection, but it will slow the spread of infection. That is why in the old days they would put salt on a wound – to slow down the infection. We are to be in the world but not of the world. We are to slow down the infection of sin. We cannot do that by retreating into our churches and church functions. We need to go where the need is. That is where our Lord will be.

Conclusion

How then shall we live?

Review: Below are four verses which we have used while working through our steps. They are significant in answering the question which many new Christians ask, "How then shall we live?" Locate the step in which these verses were first introduced, taking time to review the questions that are significant to the verse. Discuss how these verses help to answer the question, "how then shall we live?"

For my thoughts are not your thoughts, neither are your ways my ways, saith the LORD. For as the heavens are higher than the earth, so are my ways higher than your ways, and my thoughts than your thoughts. (Isaiah 55:8-9)

He hath shewed thee, O man, what is good; and what doth the LORD require of thee, but to do justly, and to love mercy, and to walk humbly with thy God? (Micah 6:8)

And be not conformed to this world: but be ye transformed by the renewing of your mind, that ye may prove what is that good, and acceptable, and perfect, will of God. (Romans 12:2)

Submitting yourselves one to another in the fear of God. (Ephesians 5:21)

Review: Below are a few helpful topics, including Bible verses, dealing with how we should live out our faith. This is not intended to be a complete list, but is intended to be a thought-provoking guide. Perhaps you will want to add some other verses to this list that you have found to be beneficial in your Christian walk.

Note: It might be helpful to review each of these topics by periodically reading these verses out loud at the end of a meeting. Try it and see how it works for your group.

With Accountability

Note: Discuss Christian accountability. This view differs from other support groups in that there are no sponsors in this program. Each person is accountable to the other members of the group to live out a true Christian witness before God.

NOTES

_____

_____

_____

_____

_____

_____

_____

_____

_____

_____

_____

_____

_____

_____

_____

_____

_____

And he looked round about on them which sat about him, and said, Behold my mother and my brethren! For whosoever shall do the will of God, the same is my brother, and my sister, and mother. (Mark 3:34-35)

As we have therefore opportunity, let us do good unto all men, especially unto them who are of the household of faith. (Galatians 6:10)

Now ye are the body of Christ, and members in particular. (1 Corinthians 12:27)

So we, being many, are one body in Christ, and every one members one of another. (Romans 12:5)

For as the body is one, and hath many members, and all the members of that one body, being many, are one body: so also is Christ. (1 Corinthians 12:12)

Ye shall not steal, neither deal falsely, neither lie one to another. (Leviticus 19:11)

Lie not one to another, seeing that ye have put off the old man with his deeds. (Colossians 3:9)

For we must all appear before the judgment seat of Christ; that every one may receive the things done in his body, according to that he hath done, whether it be good or bad. (2 Corinthians 5:10)

Whom resist stedfast in the faith, knowing that the same afflictions are accomplished in your brethren that are in the world. (1 Peter 5:9)

Fight the good fight of faith, lay hold on eternal life, whereunto thou art also called, and hast professed a good profession before many witnesses. (1 Timothy 6:12)

Thou therefore endure hardness, as a good soldier of Jesus Christ. (2 Timothy 2:3)

Iron sharpeneth iron; so a man sharpeneth the countenance of his friend. (Proverbs 27:17)

Towards Mankind

I exhort therefore, that, first of all, supplications, prayers, intercessions, and giving of thanks, be made for all men; for kings, and for all that are in authority; that we may lead a quiet and peaceable life in all godliness and honesty. For this is good and acceptable in the sight of God our Saviour. (1 Timothy 2:1-3)

Submit yourselves to every ordinance of man for the Lord's sake: whether it be to the king, as supreme; or unto governors, as unto them that are sent by him for the punishment of evildoers, and for the praise of them that do well. For so is the will of God, that with well doing ye may put to silence the ignorance of foolish men: as free, and not using your liberty for a cloke of maliciousness, but as the servants of God. (1 Peter 2:13-16)

But love ye your enemies, and do good, and lend, hoping for nothing again; and your reward shall be great, and ye shall be the children of the Highest: for he is kind unto the unthankful and to the evil. (Luke 6:35)

To the weak became I as weak, that I might gain the weak: I am made all things to all men, that I might by all means save some. (1 Corinthians 9:22)

In Deed

Beloved, follow not that which is evil, but that which is good. He that doeth good is of God: but he that doeth evil hath not seen God. (3 John 11)

Let no corrupt communication proceed out of your mouth, but that which is good to the use of edifying, that it may minister grace unto the hearers. (Ephesians 4:29)

For ye know what commandments we gave you by the Lord Jesus. For this is the will of God, even your sanctification, that ye should abstain from fornication: that every one of you should know how to possess his vessel in sanctification and honour. (1 Thessalonians 4:2-4)

That ye might walk worthy of the Lord unto all pleasing, being fruitful in every good work, and increasing in the knowledge of God. (Colossians 1:10)

Servants, be obedient to them that are your masters according to the flesh, with fear and trembling, in singleness of your heart, as unto Christ; not with eyeservice, as menpleasers; but as the servants of

Christ, doing the will of God from the heart; with good will doing service, as to the Lord, and not to men. (Ephesians 6:5-7)

And hereby we do know that we know him, if we keep his commandments. He that saith, I know him, and keepeth not his commandments, is a liar, and the truth is not in him. But whoso keepeth his word, in him verily is the love of God perfected: hereby know we that we are in him. He that saith he abideth in him ought himself also so to walk, even as he walked. (1 John 2:3-6)

If any man serve me, let him follow me; and where I am, there shall also my servant be: if any man serve me, him will my Father honour. (John 12:26)

And let us not be weary in well doing: for in due season we shall reap, if we faint not. (Galatians 6:9)

But ye, brethren, be not weary in well doing. (2 Thessalonians 3:13)

Having a good conscience; that, whereas they speak evil of you, as of evildoers, they may be ashamed that falsely accuse your good conversation in Christ. (1 Peter 3:16)

Finally, brethren, whatsoever things are true, whatsoever things are honest, whatsoever things are just, whatsoever things are pure, whatsoever things are lovely, whatsoever things are of good report; if there be any virtue, and if there be any praise, think on these things. (Philippians 4:8)

In Attitude

Rejoice evermore. Pray without ceasing. In every thing give thanks: for this is the will of God in Christ Jesus concerning you. Quench not the Spirit. (1 Thessalonians 5:16-19)

That the communication of thy faith may become effectual by the acknowledging of every good thing which is in you in Christ Jesus. (Philemon 6)

For I say, through the grace given unto me, to every man that is among you, not to think of himself more highly than he ought to think; but to think soberly, according as God hath dealt to every man the measure of faith. (Romans 12:3)

Be sober, be vigilant; because your adversary the devil, as a roaring lion, walketh about, seeking whom he may devour. (1 Peter 5:8)

For it is better, if the will of God be so, that ye suffer for well doing, than for evil doing. (1 Peter 3:17)

Whether therefore ye eat, or drink, or whatsoever ye do, do all to the glory of God. (1 Corinthians 10:31)

Who is a wise man and endued with knowledge among you? let him shew out of a good conversation his works with meekness of wisdom. (James 3:13)

With an Eye on the Eternal

That whosoever believeth in him should not perish, but have eternal life. (John 3:15)

Search the scriptures; for in them ye think ye have eternal life: and they are they which testify of me. (John 5:39)

And I give unto them eternal life; and they shall never perish, neither shall any man pluck them out of my hand. (John 10:28)

Being born again, not of corruptible seed, but of incorruptible, by the word of God, which liveth and abideth for ever. (1 Peter 1:23)

Laying up in store for themselves a good foundation against the time to come, that they may lay hold on eternal life. (1 Timothy 6:19)

For all that is in the world, the lust of the flesh, and the lust of the eyes, and the pride of life, is not of the Father, but is of the world. And the world passeth away, and the lust thereof: but he that doeth the will of God abideth for ever. (1 John 2:16-17)

Wherefore let them that suffer according to the will of God commit the keeping of their souls to him in well doing, as unto a faithful Creator. (1 Peter 4:19)

For our light affliction, which is but for a moment, worketh for us a far more exceeding and eternal weight of glory; while we look not at the things which are seen, but at the things which are not seen: for the things which are seen are temporal; but the things which are not seen are eternal. (2 Corinthians 4:17-18)

NOTES

_____
_____
_____
_____
_____
_____
_____
_____
_____
_____
_____
_____
_____
_____
_____
_____
_____

For we know that if our earthly house of this tabernacle were dissolved, we have a building of God, an house not made with hands, eternal in the heavens. (2 Corinthians 5:1)

We are confident, I say, and willing rather to be absent from the body, and to be present with the Lord. (2 Corinthians 5:8)

In a moment, in the twinkling of an eye, at the last trump: for the trumpet shall sound, and the dead shall be raised incorruptible, and we shall be changed. (1 Corinthians 15:52)

Trusting in the Lord

But my God shall supply all your need according to his riches in glory by Christ Jesus. (Philippians 4:19)

I will instruct thee and teach thee in the way which thou shalt go: I will guide thee with mine eye. (Psalm 32:8)

It is better to trust in the Lord than to put confidence in man. (Psalm 118:8)

Trust in the Lord with all thine heart; and lean not unto thine own understanding. In all thy ways acknowledge him, and he shall direct thy paths. (Proverbs 3:5-6)

Being confident of this very thing, that he which hath begun a good work in you will perform it until the day of Jesus Christ. (Philippians 1:6)

And art confident that thou thyself art a guide of the blind, a light of them which are in darkness. (Romans 2:19)

Thy word is a lamp unto my feet, and a light unto my path. (Psalm 119:105)

And thine ears shall hear a word behind thee, saying, This is the way, walk ye in it, when ye turn to the right hand, and when ye turn to the left. (Isaiah 30:21)

And we know that all things work together for good to them that love God, to them who are the called according to his purpose. (Romans 8:28)

And who is he that will harm you, if ye be followers of that which is good? (1 Peter 3:13)

What shall we then say to these things? If God be for us, who can be against us? (Romans 8:31)

The Bottom Line

Jesus said unto him, Thou shalt love the Lord thy God with all thy heart, and with all thy soul, and with all thy mind. This is the first and great commandment. And the second is like unto it, Thou shalt love thy neighbour as thyself. On these two commandments hang all the law and the prophets. (Matthew 22:37-40)

Now the end of the commandment is charity out of a pure heart, and of a good conscience, and of faith unfeigned. (1 Timothy 1:5)

And now abideth faith, hope, charity, these three; but the greatest of these is charity. (1 Corinthians 13:13)

Let us hear the conclusion of the whole matter: Fear God, and keep his commandments: for this is the whole duty of man. (Ecclesiastes 12:13)

My Scriptures

Why the King James Version?

Note: Many times while I was writing and promoting this program, people have asked me, "Why do you use the King James Version over the newer and easier-to-understand versions of the Bible?" It's important to note here that state- and county-funded and operated prisons/jails, juvenile centers, or rehabilitation centers do not promote any one version of the Bible over another. In response to that question, I have listed my own reasons below.

The KJV is probably the only translation with which no parties involved had an ax to grind. Too many churches today are promoting doctrines that are antithetical to the Word of God. The translation of the King James Version was a national undertaking back in the 1600s in which no one had any special interest at heart, save that of producing the best possible version of the Scriptures. The first edition of the Greek text to be published was that from Desiderius Erasmus. It was printed in 1516 and was used by Martin Luther for his German translation. Erasmus also published editions in 1522, 1527, and 1535. Fifteen years later, in 1550, Robert Stephens published his edition, known as the royal edition, which adhered to the text of the 1527 and 1535 editions of Erasmus. In 1565, Theodore Beza published his edition in Geneva, based largely upon Stephens' text. The editions of Erasmus, Stephens, and Beza (particularly that of 1598) were the chief sources used for the translation of the King James Version of 1611.

The King James Bible is the most beautiful, beloved, and popular English translation to date. It has an established history and has changed many lives for the better. It is the Bible version from which John Newton, Samuel Rutherford, John Wesley, Charles Finney, Dwight Moody, Charles Spurgeon, Billy Sunday, Billy Graham, and so many other men of faith preached with power. If it was good enough for them, certainly it is good enough for me.

While newer versions use modern English, I believe something is lost in the modernization. I attended a funeral at which a pastor read Psalm 23 from the New International Version of the Bible. To me, that reading seemed diluted and lacking. I would feel the same (to a lesser degree) if someone would read Shakespeare to me in modern English. This also caused me to ask how many simplified versions of the Bible are needed before it is rendered simple enough. Many who have studied the English language have written with great concern about how the language has been *dumbed down*. Must we dumb down the Bible as well?

While teaching a Bible study in an Ohio prison, I noticed that one inmate (who liked to read) was struggling with reading the KJV. The struggle was so manifest that one day after class I pulled him aside and mentioned that there were simpler versions of the Bible that he could read while he worked his way up to the King James Version. You can imagine how convicted I was when he replied, "Sir, you don't have to dumb this book down for me; I will step up to this book." On his final day in class, just prior to his release, he read an entire passage from his King James Bible without making a single mistake. For this he received a heartwarming ovation from his classmates. The smile and look of accomplishment on this inmate's face were very rewarding to me, and I have never mentioned to anyone else that they might want to read a simpler version of the Bible.

Another thing I have thought about and will share with you here is this: one day in the not-so-distant future, we will be summoned to appear in a courtroom and defend those things we believe. Our defense will be that we stand on the Word of God. I can envision the prosecuting attorney bringing in wheelbarrow after wheelbarrow of various translations of the Bible and asking the question, "Which one of these is the Word of God?"

Someone on our side will say, "The NIV."

Another will answer, "The American Standard Version."

Others might answer, "The Amplified Version," or "The Living Bible," and so on, until the argument that we are standing on the Word of God becomes so diminished and confused that our claim will be thrown out.

To make matters worse some of the newer versions of the Bible omit up to forty-five verses in the New Testament, either in the footnotes or from the text itself, that are otherwise found in the KJV. Some words that have been changed have missed the intended meaning. For example, *longsuffering* has been replaced with *patience*. It takes patience to be longsuffering, but the point is, the one doing the longsuffering is in the right and responds to a wrong by giving the wrongdoer an opportunity to repent.

During one of my classes at a ladies' recovery center in Georgia, one of the ladies read Psalm 3 from her version of the Bible. The word *salvation* in the last verse of the Psalm was replaced with the word *victory*, totally missing the point. Another example is the word *fear* in some versions is replaced with *reverential awe*, which represents about 25 percent of the word's intended meaning. These are just a few examples that cause me to favor the King James Version.

Now I come to the most important reason: the King James Version was translated from the *Textus Receptus* (Latin for *Received Text*). Although the KJV was not translated from the earliest Greek texts, it was translated from the Majority Text – the *Textus Receptus*, the preserved text of God. (See Psalm 12:6-7, Matthew 5:18, and Luke 11:51.) I think it is important to realize that *earlier* is not a synonym for *reliable*. An earlier text could be flawed, depending on who did the translating and from what that translation had been copied. So, it is the King James for me! I love it. I love to read it and I love to hear it being read. I even love the feel of it when I hold it in my hand. God is good.

The End is Better than the Beginning

Several years ago, I was invited to preach at my home church on Father's Day. I was blessed to see many of my family members and friends in attendance. One of those in attendance was my granddaughter, Tayah. Tayah likes to draw, and while I was speaking, she was making me a Father's Day card. She handed that card to me after the service while I was on my way to the back of the church to shake hands with people. In between handshakes, I glanced at the card. Although I still have that card safely stowed away, I cannot remember the picture she had drawn on it, but I will never forget the words she had written. Her message simply said, "Happy Father's Day, Grandpa. You are a great preacher and I love you! Tayah" I adore that girl! As I read what she had written, my knees buckled as I realized that God was using Tayah's words to show me how far He had taken me. Do you remember the letter I received from Stephanie while I was in prison? The card I received from Tayah was God taking me full circle. My life had been restored.

I shared a story while I was in Africa (and I have used it many times since) that ties in with the Father's Day account I shared above. I don't know if this story is true, but if it is not, it should be. It goes like this: In England during the olden days, a person caught stealing was branded with a *T* so that everyone would know he was a thief. Two brothers were caught stealing sheep and were branded on both hands with an *ST*, which stood for *sheep thief*.

One brother became very bitter and played the blame-shifting game. He blamed his parents, his education, his peers, and his neighborhood for making him the way he was. I am quite convinced that if they had known about genetics then, he would have blamed his genes. He never took responsibility for his own decisions, and as a result, he became angrier and angrier at society. He drank heavily, and before long he was a full-blown, miserable alcoholic. He also became a loner, a recluse, who hated people in general. This man eventually died from alcohol poisoning at the age of forty-three. No one attended his funeral, and he was buried in an unmarked grave.

The other brother, however, took responsibility for what he had done. He acknowledged that he had sinned and was in need of God's forgiveness. He called on Jesus to save him and was born again. He studied his Bible and became active in the church. He was a man people of all ages came to know and to love. When he died at the ripe old age of ninety-three, people came from hundreds of miles to pay their last respects to this precious man of God. One of these was his great-great granddaughter. While standing before the casket with her mother, she looked at the crossed hands of the deacon and asked, "Mother, what are those *ST*s on great-great grandfather's hands?"

Her mother replied, "I don't know child; I have often wondered that myself, but I believe they stand for *saint*."

God can certainly change a life. I know, because He changed mine. My granddaughter Tayah is not going to remember me as a three-time convicted felon. She is going to remember that her grandfather preached the Word of God, that he fed orphans in Africa, and that he took presents to children on Christmas whose parents were in prison. She is going to remember that her grandfather taught in prisons and recovery centers. She is going to remember that her grandfather loved people so much that he shared Jesus with them. This is the hope I have for those who take this program. I pray that you will turn away from your life of addiction and embrace the person you could be in Christ.

Addenda

Breaking it Down

Ephesians 5:21: (1) Submitting yourselves one to another (2) in the fear of God.

Submit = (A) *hupŏtassō* (Strong's #5293). Combination of Greek word (B) *hupŏ* (Strong's #5259): under status of authority, and (C) *tassō* (Strong's #5021): to arrange or determine. We determine to place ourselves under some authority or person. (D) Combined = subject or subjection.

In the above, A = B + C or A = D.

(1) Submit = Subject = one who is under the rule of another or others, especially one who owes allegiance to a government or ruler.

Allegiance = loyalty, as to a cause; the obligation of a vassal to his lord.

Vassal = one who holds land for a feudal lord; a bondman or slave.

Loyalty = faithful to one's allegiance, as to a government or friends.

Faithful = steady in allegiance or affection; true to a fact or a standard; reliable.

Rely/Reliable = to confidently depend on/to be dependable.

Depend = to place trust in; to rely on for aid and support.

Trust = firm reliance on the integrity (adherence to a strict ethical code), ability, or character of a person or thing.

Aid = to help or assist (to help or support).

Support = to keep from giving way; to sustain a person under affliction; to uphold or advocate; to corroborate.

Sustain = to provide with the necessities of existence.

Uphold = to lift upward.

Advocate = one who pleads for or on behalf of another.

Corroborate = to strengthen or support with evidence; to make certain.

(2) Fear = phŏbŏs (Strong's #5401): combination of: (a) fear, (b) terror, (c) respect, and (d) reverence.

Fear/Terror

Fear = a distressing emotion aroused by impending danger, evil, or pain. Distressing = a state of extreme necessity or misfortune; causing anxiety, pain, sorrow.

Emotion = a strong feeling.

Arouse = to awaken, stir up, excite.

Impending = about to happen; a threat.

Terror = intense fear.

Intense = existing in a high extreme or degree; acute or vehement emotions.

Acute = sharp or severe; extremely serious, critical.

Vehement = forceful or intense in expression, emotion, or conviction.

Critical = constituting a crisis.

Crisis = a turning point for the better or worse; a period of instability.

Respect/Reverence

Respect = esteem, admiration, proper courtesy.

Esteem = respect, admiration.

Admiration = to regard with pleasure, approval, and often, wonder; to regard highly.

Regard = to look at in a particular way.

Pleasure = enjoyment or satisfaction.

Enjoyment = to have the use or benefit of.

Satisfaction = a source of contentment or fulfillment; to meet all needs or requirements.

Proper courtesy = appropriate, correct, fitting, right; showing good manners; polite.

Appropriate = suitable.

Correct = true, accurate; in accordance with an acknowledged standard; free from error.

Manners = a way of doing or being done.

Polite = showing good manners; courteous.

Reverence = a feeling of profound awe, respect, and often, love.

Awe = a mixed emotion of respect, dread, and wonder; inspired, as by authority, genius, great beauty, or might.

Fruit of the Spirit (Galatians 5:22-23)

Love (Strong's #26): agapē (ag-ah'-pay)

> The active love of God for His Son and His people, and the active love His people are to have for Him. A sacrificial love expressed, expecting nothing in return, extended even toward one's enemies.

Joy (Strong's #5479): chara (khar-ah')

> Cheerfulness expressed by rejoicing, calm delight, gladness.

Peace (Strong's #1515): ĕirēnē (i-rah'-nay)

> Quietness, rest, implied prosperity, tranquility, lack of strife, a reconciled condition.

Longsuffering (Strong's #3115): makrŏthumia (mak-roth-oo-mee'-ah)

> Forbearance, patience; internal and external control in a difficult circumstance, which control could exhibit itself by delaying an action.

Gentleness (Strong's #5544): chrēstŏtēs (khray-stot'-ace)

> Moral excellence in character and demeanor; the active expression of kindness and goodness.

Goodness (Strong's #19) agathōsunē (ag-ath-o-soo'-nay)

> Being positive or desirable in nature; morally correct, worthy of respect, honorable, beneficial, well-behaved, obedient.

Faith (Strong's #4102): pistis (pis'-tis)

> Belief or trust, implying that actions based upon that belief or trust should follow; confident belief in the truth; value or trustworthiness of a person, idea, or thing; a belief that does not rest on logical truth or material evidence.

Meekness (Strong's #4236): praŏtēs (prah-ot'-ace)

> Gentleness, humility, courtesy, considerateness; the positive quality of dealing with people in a kind manner, with humility and consideration.

Temperance (Strong's #1466): ĕgkratĕia (eng-krat'-i-ah)

> Self-control; logical dominion over one's desire, emotions, instincts.

Works of the Flesh (Galatians 5:19-21)

Adultery (Strong's #3430): mŏichĕia (moy-khi'-ah)

> Voluntary sexual intercourse between a married person and a partner other than a lawful spouse.

Fornication (Strong's #4202): pŏrnĕia (por-ni'-ah)

> Sexual immorality; a general term for sexual sin of any kind. Primarily used to describe sexual relations between unmarried couples.

Uncleanness (Strong's #167): akatharsia (ak-ath-ar-see'-ah)

> A state of moral filthiness, especially in relation to sexual sin.

Lasciviousness (Strong's #766): asĕlgĕia (as-elg'-i-a)

> Extreme indulgence in sensual pleasure; lewd, immoral; marked by unprovoked maliciousness.

Idolatry (Strong's #1495): ĕidōlŏlatrĕia (i-do-lol-at-ri'-ah)

> Worshipping an object or image of a false god; blind or excessive devotion to something; allowing something to take precedence over God.

Witchcraft (Strong's #5331): pharmakĕia (far-mak-i'-ah)

> Magic; the use of spells or potions of magic, often involving drugs; use of supernatural powers over people by calling on spirits for aid (sorcery).

Hatred (Strong's #2189): ĕchthra (ekh'-thrah)

> Intense dislike or distaste for a person, place, or thing; to feel hostility towards.

Variance (Strong's #2054): ĕris (er'-is)

> Quarrels, strife, dissension, contention, discord.

Emulations (Strong's #2205): zēlŏs (dzay'-los)

Effort or ambition to equal or excel another, especially through intimidation; imitation of another.

Wrath (Strong's #2372): thumŏs (thoo-mos')

Fury, anger, rage; a state of intense displeasure in some real or perceived wrong.

Strife (Strong's #2052): ĕrithĕia (er-ith-i'-ah)

Heated, often violent dissension, especially as a result of selfish ambition; a struggle, fight, or quarrel.

Seditions (Strong's #1370): dichŏstasia (dee-khos-tas-ee'-ah)

Conduct or language inciting a rebellion against the authority of a state or governing body.

Heresies (Strong's #139): hairĕsis (hah'ee-res-is)

Opinions or doctrines at variance with established religious beliefs.

Envyings (Strong's #5355): phthŏnŏs (fthon'-os)

Feelings of discontent and resentment aroused by the desire for the possessions or qualities of another.

Murders (Strong's #5408): phŏnŏs (fon'-os)

Unlawful killings, slaughter.

Drunkenness (Strong's #3178): mĕthē (meth'-ay)

Intoxicated with alcoholic liquor to the point of impairment of physical and mental faculties.

Revellings (Strong's #2970): kōmŏs (ko'-mos)

Rowdy behavior, partying, orgy; boisterous merrymaking, carousing.

Basic Bible Exercise

Note: Many of the individuals attending the meetings will have no familiarity with the Bible. They will not have a church background. This exercise is helpful in teaching them how to use our *Owner's Manual and Guide*. Those who know their Bibles should not be offended by this basic review. They must understand that there is a need for this type of exercise.

The best way to conduct this exercise is to get everyone involved by using the question-and-answer format. This should be kept simple. Here is an example:

The Bible is one book with how many parts?

What are those two parts? (Old Testament/New Testament)

Is the Old Testament found in the front or the back of the Bible?

Is the New Testament found in the front or the back of the Bible?

Are both parts of the Bible relevant today?

The Old Testament was originally written in what language? (Hebrew)

The New Testament was originally written in what language? (Greek)

What was the Greek translation of the Jewish Scriptures called? (Septuagint)

What was the translation of the Old and New Testaments into Latin called? (Vulgate)

The two parts of the Bible are broken down into what? (Books)

What are the names of some books in the Old Testament?

What are the names of some books in the New Testament?

The books are broken down into what? (Chapters)

The chapters are broken down into what? (Verses)

The verses are broken down into what? (Sub-verses, e.g. a, b, c)

Find John 3:16.

About the Author

My name is Larry Skrant. Before that I was 324-242. Before that I was 282-320. And before that I was 230-915. Those are prison numbers. To the state of Ohio, I was a three-time loser. To society, I was beyond salvaging. To all, including myself, I was beyond hope. Then I met Christ, and He gave me a new heart and a new life. I am now a member of the First Baptist Church in Spencer, Ohio, an ordained minister, the director of Changed Lives Ministries, and the founder of Addicts at the Cross. God changes the unchangeable.

To learn more, or if interested in working with Changed Lives Ministries, visit:

www.changedlivesministries.org

9 Steps – Addicts at the Cross

1. Admit – I admit that my life is not my own and is beyond my ability to manage or control. I have become powerless over the substance or substances that I have abused. I acknowledge my need for God to set me free from all the things in this world that have me ensnared and prevent me from being the person God created me to be.

2. Believe – I believe that the God I need to restore my life and make me whole is to be found in the person of Jesus Christ, the Word who was with God, who is God, and who became flesh and dwelt among us (John 1:1, 14).

3. Decide – I have decided to turn from the things of the past (repent) and to ask Jesus to be lord and manager of my life (surrender).

4. Search – I have made an honest search and moral inventory of myself, and seek to eliminate that which is not in accord with God's will for my life.

5. Acknowledge – Before God, others, and myself, I acknowledge my inventory to be true. I now begin to use the information from my inventory, formulating a plan that will result in a life set free from addiction.

6. Change – I am willing to change and to allow God to change me.

7. Ask – I humbly ask God to forgive me and to change me through the power of His Holy Spirit.

8. Restore – I have made a list of all the people my actions have or may have affected/ damaged, and I ask myself, "How can I make this right?"

9. Pursue – Daily, I seek to know and live out God's will, plan, and purpose for my life.

Made in the USA
Middletown, DE
26 January 2018